Secret Stories of Extinct Disneyland

Memories of the Original Park

Jim Korkis

Theme Park Press

The Happiest Books on Earth

www.ThemeParkPress.com

Theme Park Press publishes its books in a variety of print and electronic formats. Some content that appears in one format may not appear in another.

Editor: Bob McLain
Layout: Artisanal Text

ISBN 979-8-89609-060-1
Printed in the United States of America

Theme Park Press | www.ThemeParkPress.com
Address queries to ben@themeparkpress.com

*Dedicated to my brothers Michael and Chris who experienced
extinct Disneyland with me although their memories
of it are sometimes as faded by time as mine.*

CONTENTS

Introduction

In a 1956 interview with writer Pete Martin of *The Saturday Evening Post,* Walt Disney stated:

> Disneyland means a lot to me in that it's something that will never be finished. Something that I can keep developing; keep "plussing" and adding to. It will be a live, breathing thing that will need changes.

Disneyland has constantly changed from the moment it first opened with Walt himself almost immediately adding things and removing others.

Over six decades, even some iconic attractions have changed in significant ways. The Matterhorn no longer has a Skyway passing through its upper level but it now includes a menacing Abominable Snowman stalking its glacial caverns. The Pirates of the Caribbean now showcases additions from the popular movie franchise.

Some attractions have disappeared completely but sometimes elements of them can still be located in the attractions that replaced them. Items from the long gone Mine Train Through Nature's Wonderland can be still discovered scattered beside the tracks of the Big Thunder Mountain Railroad. The ship's bell, seashell planter and chest from the Swiss Family Treehouse are now part of the décor of Tarzan's Treehouse as is the familar sound of the "Swisskapolka."

Some things are removed because of maintenance or safety issues. Some things are removed because of lack of capacity as attendance has grown. Some things are removed because guests just stopped wanting to visit because of changing tastes. Some things are removed to save money.

I am old enough that I actually experienced much of extinct Disneyland personally although in some cases I was too young to fully appreciate or clearly remember some of those experiences. I vaguely recall being uneasy riding on the back of a pack mule, puzzled at trying to figure out the time on the Clock of the World and very frightened when a Haunted Mansion suit of armor lunged out toward my doombuggy.

On the other hand, I can still clearly recall Wally Boag performing as Pecos Bill, or rocking underneath a support tower on a Skyway bucket, and struggling to adjust my weight so that I could shift my flying saucer to bump into my brothers as if I had just experienced those things yesterday.

Disney has shown itself to be notoriously poor in proper documentation especially of the early years of Disneyland. Opening and closing dates, proper nomenclature and more are the best I could verify from multiple sources including my own interviews with Imagineers.

This is not a definitive listing of all things missing at Disneyland and even as this book is being published other favorites are disappearing. Hopefully, what is here will bring back fond memories for some people while at the same time sparking the curiosity of those people who never experienced them at all.

—Jim Korkis
Disney Historian
April 2019

Main Street, U.S.A.

Disney lessees are today known as operating participants. Disneyland General Manager C.V. Wood was the person responsible for getting a variety of companies to lease space inside the park and even pay their own construction costs, create their own exhibits and often staff their own area. WED Enterprises (Imagineering) still had to supervise and approve the work.

Showcasing their product and tying their name to the magic of the Disney brand was enough incentive for many businesses. In return, Disneyland was able to provide additional experiences for the guests without having to pay for all of it.

The use of lessees was particularly prominent on Main Street, U.S.A. and Tomorrowland and accounts for many changes as businesses discovered they were not getting the value for their investment and left. In addition, as the first five year leases began to run out, Disneyland decided not to renew them and often took over the running of the location.

On Main Street, Grandma's Baby Shop disappeared within the first few months and was soon followed by other shops including Jimmy Starr's Show Business Souvenirs store and the Maxwell House Coffee Shop. Businesses were constantly disappearing and replaced by other businesses that also vanished.

Bandstand

JULY 1955—1962

Walt Disney grew up in Marceline, Missouri where in E.P. Ripley Park there was a gazebo that served as a stage after church services for Sunday band concerts. Walt's family would spend the afternoon sitting on a quilt spread on the ground listening to the music.

Imagineer Herb Ryman drew some concept sketches of the bandstand in Town Square in 1954 and early construction photos show it being built there. It was Walt's intention that guests entering the park would be greeted by the Disneyland Band playing music.

The image of the bandstand in that location appears on early merchandise and marketing materials. Walt felt that the gazebo structure could also be used for ceremonies since it stood above the crowd.

However, as the park was being built, it became apparent that the size of the structure was obstructing the view of Main Street and in particular Sleeping Beauty Castle. It was roughly fifteen feet tall not counting the small flagpole on top. It had a short staircase, decorative railings and finials and was painted white with red trim.

So, before opening day, it was moved to the hub area between the entrances of Fantasyland and Frontierland.

As expected, the bandstand proved popular as the band played every day to guests sitting on park benches. In fact, it was so popular that Walt decided to have Imagineer John Hench expand the area into a dance pavilion called Carnation Plaza Gardens that opened August 1956 to handle the crowds and encourage guests to stay later in the park.

The bandstand was relocated to a section of land at the intersection of Adventureland and Frontierland that was dubbed Magnolia Park where it would remain for six more years. Besides the band concerts, it became home to the Christmas Bowl holiday performances as well as events like the Kal-Kan Kennel dog shows.

When the Jungle Cruise expanded in 1962, there was no room for the bandstand and Walt donated it to the City of Anaheim in hopes it would find a new home in some local park.

The original Roger's Gardens center opened in 1965 by Roger McKinnon in Costa Mesa. Gavin Herbert Sr. bought the business in January 1970 and five years later moved it to its current location in Corona del Mar.

Herbert had well known relationships with many of Orange County's elite including connections with Disney. He was alerted by the City of Anaheim that they intended to trash the bandstand that was still in storage. Herbert sent a big truck up the next day and had it hauled to Roger's Gardens.

The bandstand is now within the Farmhouse restaurant at Roger's Gardens. Its light bulbs have been removed and the paint sanded back to the original wood but is still recognizable.

The Dixieland Bandstand that jetted out over the Rivers of America provided a location for musicians and a place for guests to enjoy shade and scenery when there were no performances. When construction began on New Orleans Square, it too disappeared.

Bank of America

JULY 1955—JULY 1993

Bank of America had been a long time supporter of Walt Disney beginning with its help in financing *Snow White and the Seven Dwarfs* (1937) and then later Disney animated features including *Pinocchio, Bambi, Dumbo,* and *Cinderella*. It also supplied loans to help build Disneyland and later Walt Disney World.

The thirty-five foot long bank building located to the far right on the first floor of the Opera House in Town Square was a functioning bank used by the guests, Disneylanders (to cash their checks whether they had an account there or not) and lessees for business transactions. For many years, it was the only bank in the United States to be open on a Sunday or holidays.

"In the unique, old-fashioned atmosphere of this branch, you may find it hard to believe that it is a fully-equipped, completely modern banking office! Yet that's why we're here—to be your bank away from home!" stated "Your Guide to Disneyland," a complimentary, color brochure map of the park produced by Bank of America for guests who stopped by the branch. The first edition was published in 1955 with continuing updates over the years.

Walt located an original 1904 bank vault from the Mosler Safe Company and had it installed inside the building where it still exists today. It was originally air-tight but that changed when Bank of America left.

The interior of the building had hardwood teller windows, a brass hat rack, shiny cuspidors, an old fashioned settee with matching chair, a roll top desk for the manager, and an 1880 typewriter still in working order. Tellers were dressed in vests and string ties.

The bank also offered collectible souvenir money orders in dollar (with the side image of a steam train engine), five dollar (image of the front of the Disneyland Bank of America) and ten dollar denominations (a sidewheeler riverboat, not the *Mark Twain*, since it was based on early concept art) convertible into cash at banks and stores everywhere. In 2008, one of the one dollar money orders sold on eBay for $306.

The bank also provided the option of opening a real bank account and being eligible to get checks with Disneyland images of them.

When the park first opened, the business hours were 11 a.m. to 5 p.m. but the hours later adjusted to 10 a.m. to 4:00 p.m., the traditional "banker's hours".

When Bank of America ended its sponsorship of the It's A Small World attraction, it also stopped its participation as a working bank. For eight years the bank was renamed Bank of Main Street (which required special permission from the state banking commission since it no longer operated as a bank) but was primarily an information center and Annual Pass Center although it did exchange currency and cash small checks. It eventually closed in 2009 and reopened as the Disney Gallery.

Upjohn Pharmacy

JULY 1955—SEPTEMBER 1970

Walt was good friends with Donald S. Gilmore, chairman of the board and managing director of Upjohn, a large pharmaceutical manufacturer since 1886. They later became Pfizer.

The main section of the shop was a reproduction of an old-time apothecary shop based on three New York pharmacies that were in existence before 1886. The other section was a contemporary display showing phases of then present day pharmaceutical manufacturing as well as a large aerial photo of the Upjohn Portage plant with descriptive captions.

It was not a real pharmacy even though two real pharmacists (Fredrick August Eckstein and Philip Milton Harvey) were in the shop to answer guests' questions.

The shop gave away free postcards as well as a free square miniature glass bottle of orange-flavored Unicap Vitamins, inside a red box with a white silhouette of the Disneyland castle logo and a pamphlet containing a history of the Upjohn company. The bottle was an inch and a half tall and contained twelve vitamins.

From *The Overflow*, the monthly Upjohn sales magazine, April 1955:

> Our only reason for sponsoring the store is that its presence in Disneyland constitutes sound, inexpensive, advertising with exciting possibilities. As Disney reaps the profits of his latest work, Upjohn will get full advertising value.
>
> Year after year, Disneyland will present the name Upjohn to the public, much as an ad in *Life* magazine presents the Company's name. But an ad in *Life* does the job once. Disneyland does it many times.

Garrard MacLeod, M.D., editor of *Scope* magazine and an antiquer by avocation helped in the historical research and the procurement of the some four hundred authentic pieces of apothecary equipment. Eventually, it grew to over a thousand items.

The stove from 1900 was found in a New Jersey shop. The leaded glass chandeliers came from the attic of a Kalamazoo druggist who bought them in the 1890s and used them in his shop until 1918. The herb grinder at the time was seventy-five years old.

A collection of antique microscopes dating back to the 1700s were purchased from a New York collector. Dr. MacLeod fixed some of the parts so that each was usable and vintage slides were included. There was a collection of syringes dating from 1850.

Glass jars filled with live leeches were on display. At the turn of the century, they were used to draw blood from infected parts of the body. Many of the original artifacts from the Upjohn Disneyland Pharmacy are in the Pharmacy Museum at the University of Arizona in Tucson.

There remains a hanging sign on Main Street that advertises "Rx Drugs" (Rx being the medieval symbol of "to take") in honor of the Upjohn Pharmacy. A window above the Fortuosity Shop (Upjohn's former location) lists "D. S. Gilmore, MD and E.G. Upjohn, MD." Dr. E. G. Upjohn was the grandson of co-founder Dr. Henry Upjohn and chairman and president of Upjohn Pharmaceuticals during the 1950s and 1960s.

Wurlitzer Music Hall

JULY 1955—SEPTEMBER 1968

Located on the northeast corner of Town Square was the huge Wurltizer Music Hall that was a glamorous showroom displaying beautiful pianos and organs. In keeping with the spirit of Main Street, U.S.A. at the turn-of-the-century, mechanical player pianos performed traditional tunes as well.

The Rudolph Wurlitzer Company was founded in 1853, and was especially famous for its theatre organs and juke boxes. Having its store on Main Street gave a legitimacy of the appropriate era to Walt Disney's park. The company went out of business in 1988.

Wurlitzer claimed that it was "The Name That Means Music In Disneyland."

Besides the contemporary pianos and organs offered for sale by Wurlitzer, the shop exhibited a 1838 Harp Piano and a 1905 Piananino. There was also a piano key wired to an oscilloscope so when a guest hit the key, they could see the wave pattern of the note as an oscillating green beam of light on the scanner screen.

Guests could purchase sheet music and even player piano rolls in the wide open space that had a checkerboard tile floor and lots of live potted plants.

The Wurlitzer company took out a full page, full color magazine advertisement claiming "every piano and organ at Disneyland is a Wurlitzer...make your home a wonderland of music too!" In the earliest years of Disneyland, the claim that all the pianos and organs were Wurlitzers was true.

Of course, guests were not going to purchase a piano at the park and take it home. However, they could window-shop in this showcase and an employee could take their information for a follow-up from their hometown store.

Electric organs were promoted as easy to learn and so demonstrations encouraged shoppers to consider buying one. Sometimes free lessons were also in the package. Wurlitzer hoped that people might buy an organ or a piano because they heard them played beautifully and effortlessly all throughout the day by its employees. In addition, the foot traffic at the front of Disneyland supplied many more potential buyers than the usual local store.

The general manager of the store was Dee Fisher. In the evening, as the park was closing, he would sit down at a Wurlitzer electric organ and play songs from Disney movies like *Bambi, Peter Pan, Cinderella, So Dear To My Heart,* and *Lady and the Tramp.* The departing crowd would gather outside the shop to stop and listen. Many considered it a goodbye kiss from Disneyland.

These informal concerts were so popular that Disneyland Records did an album of Fisher playing his Disneyland repertoire that was recorded at Disneyland to try to capture the feeling of this twilight treat. It was released in 1957 and entitled *Echoes of Disneyland.*

Fisher was quite an accomplished performer who appeared in venues throughout the West and had just returned from a gig in the Hawaiian Islands when he recorded the songs for this album.

The Intimate Apparel Shop
JULY 1955—JANUARY 1956

One of Disneyland's General Manager C.V. Wood's personal friends was Herndon Norris who was president of the Hollywood-Maxwell Brassiere Company in Los Angeles established twenty-one years earlier, which is why Norris got a lease for a shop on Main Street since Wood had to approve all park lessees.

Walt Disney apparently disliked the idea of a corset shop when it was pitched to him but relented in order to fill out Main Street with businesses especially since a historical exhibit would be included.

Herndon proudly proclaimed his business to be "the largest bra manufacturer west of the Mississippi" with ten plants in America, one in Canada and multiple licensing contracts with companies overseas.

It was the only shop on Main Street with an outside front porch and three small steps to enter inside. The reason has been debated including that it prevented children from looking directly into the showroom and that it provided a place for men to wait while women shopped for their under garments.

Half of the shop was an exhibit on the history of under garments but guests could actually buy current 1955 corsets and bras in the other half that was referred to as the "corseteria." The interior of the shop resembled a Victorian "front-room" complete with period fireplace, drapes, large mirror, sofa and old-fashioned showcase.

The history section featured an authentic 1860s Singer Sewing Machine. There were also small model 3-D "illusion" boxes using lenticular technology that featured women attired in turn of the century clothing from one angle but as you moved your head to a different angle it transformed into them wearing just the corsets and pantaloons of their era. The modern era had them transform from evening wear to bra and petticoat which often prompted embarrassed giggling.

The main attraction was an exhibit hosted by the Wizard of Bras, the mascot of the Hollywood-Maxwell company. In the exhibit, he was a mechanical figure with an approximately minute and a half tape-recorded spiel on a revolving stage. One side was a complete re-creation of the fashions and intimate wear of the 1890s and on the other side was a showing of the inner and outer wear fashions of 1955 emphasizing the superiority of Hollywood-Maxwell's products.

The shop closed within the first months because people did not come to Disneyland to buy intimate apparel despite Hollywood-Maxwell having a good reputation for supplying "who-can-tells" (handmade full false breasts) to Hollywood leading ladies to enhance their glamorous silhouettes.

When the store closed in 1956, the Ruggles China and Glass Shop that was next door expanded into that space.

In 1958, the Hollywood-Maxwell Company of California merged with the Vassar Company of Chicago (operated by Munsingwear). The result was the Hollywood Vassarette Intimate Apparel Division. At one time, Munsingwear was America's prominent underwear provider.

Story Book Shop
JULY 1955—APRIL 1995

Due to its long association with Disney beginning in 1933, Western Printing and Lithographing didn't hesitate to invest $200,000 (a considerable sum in the mid-1950s) in the creation of Disneyland, Inc. giving them 13.8 percent of Walt's new theme park.

Western Printing and Lithographing was the parent company of Whitman Publishing and Simon & Schuster, Inc.

Western considered it an outstanding partnership because in the process it provided the rights to unlimited merchandising potential of the Disneyland name for its own products as well as providing the benefit to Disneyland of using Western's printing presses and expertise to produce high-quality press kits, guide maps, brochures, menus, premiums and much more for Walt's new park, with the added benefit of refreshing some of that same material on a frequent basis.

In addition, Western ran the Story Book Shop, sometimes called the Arcade Bookstore, on Main Street. It provided a significant "billboard" that the Western-produced line of Dell comics were tied directly to the family-friendly wholesome world of Disney.

This was important at a time when comic books were coming under heavy scrutiny including congressional hearings linking comic books to juvenile delinquency and reduced sales as people found other entertainment sources like television.

It was a small space located officially in the Crystal Arcade just behind the Upjohn Pharmacy. There was an entry through the Emporium and also from West Center Street across from the Carnation Ice Cream Parlor and the Flower Mart. Its three walls were completely filled with comic books.

It was very unusual to have a shop dedicated to comic books since they were generally sold on spinner racks in grocery stores, drug stores, and newsstands.

In the early years, Disney Dell comic books were also sold at the newsstand out by the ticket kiosks at the entrance.

The store also had a huge assortment of Western-produced publications including sticker books, coloring books, Little Golden Books and more that filled several tables. When it came to comic books, it was not unusual to see the current issue of Dell's *Tarzan* or *The Lone Ranger* next to a copy of an adaptation of *Lady and the Tramp* or the latest issue of *Uncle Scrooge*.

By 1960, Disney bought back Western's investment in the park that essentially ended Western's participation including creating special Disneyland themed comic books.

The shop disappeared because of the 1995 remodel of the Crystal Arcade and has since become merely an extension of the Emporium selling the same usual Disneyland merchandise.

In a special June 1954 ceremony, Walt Disney himself purchased the two and a half billionth Dell comic for ten cents. Dell Comics Distinguished Achievement Award 1956 was presented to Walt Disney on January 15, 1957 "in appreciation of his continuous and significant contributions in combining so successfully the fields of entertainment and education for American youth." It is currently on display at the Walt Disney Family Museum in San Francisco.

Sunkist Citrus House

JULY 1960—JANUARY 1989

Nearly 160 acres of citrus trees had to be cleared to build Disneyland. The oranges grown on the property over the years were sold to Sunkist, the largest shipper of fresh produce in the U.S.

Sunkist marketed its fresh-squeezed fruit juice as a healthy alternative to artificial beverages like Coca-Cola.

The Sunkist Citrus House took over the former location of the Puffin Bakery. The former bakery's dining room was enlarged by taking over the adjacent space that had been previously operated by Sunny-View Farms Jams and Jellies.

While the interior space was now one large dining area with tables and chairs and the counter on the far left, the exterior still looked like two separate businesses. It was later replaced by the Blue Ribbon Bakery and eventually the Gibson Girl Ice Cream Parlor.

Two years later, another beverage location also opened in Adventureland named Sunkist, I Presume (referencing Stanley's famous first words to Dr. Livingstone in darkest Africa) that also served the same Sunkist products. It was later replaced by Bengal Barbeque in 1992.

The shops were owned by the Perricone Citrus Company (Sam Perricone) and run by B.C. "Bo" Foster. Guests could have fresh citrus shipped anywhere in the United States in a special Disneyland box. Orange juice was fresh squeezed every day at Disneyland for both the Citrus House and Adventureland location as well as distributed to all the restaurants in the park.

In addition to fresh squeezed orange juice from oranges and lemonade from concentrate as well as frozen fruit juice bars, the shop sold lemon tarts, lemon meringue pie and orange cheesecake from Marcheta's Bakery in Garden Grove.

Every day, employees drove to Yorba Linda to get the oranges, to Corona to pick up the large containers of frozen lemonade concentrate and to Garden Grove for the pastries. The shop also made the non-alcoholic Mint Julep (orange juice, lemonade, mint flavoring, sugar and grenadine syrup) sold on the *Mark Twain* at the time.

The main attraction of the Citrus House was the semi-automatic juice squeezers where an employee had to constantly feed the oranges one at a time into the chute on top of the squeezer. They used size 138 oranges, meaning an average size so that 138 oranges fit into a single carton. Only Valencia oranges were used, never navel oranges.

The machine automatically cut them in half and squeezed the juice with six reamers on one side and six on the other. The reamers slowly rotated around, picked up an orange half, squeezed it, and dumped the peel in a circular motion with a continuous stream of juice trickling out.

Walt was fascinated by the machine and often in the early morning hours before the park opened, he would unlock the shop and make himself a glass of orange juice, often inviting workmen he found on the street to join him so he could keep using the machine. Eventually, he was given a small version for his Disneyland apartment.

The Walt Disney Story
APRIL 1973—FEBRUARY 1975

The Legacy of Walt Disney, a tribute to Disneyland's founder, that was exhibited in the corner Town Square shop in what was the former Wurtlizer Music Hall from January 1970 to February 1973 found much of that material moved to the Main Street Opera House. It was replaced by Disneyland Presents a Preview of Coming Attractions exhibit.

The Walt Disney Story in the 500 seat Opera House that opened April 8, 1973, featured everything "from Mickey Mouse to the Magic Kingdoms and is presented free by Gulf Oil" at a time when Disneyland still used ticket coupons. It replaced the Great Moments with Mr. Lincoln attraction and many guests were vocally disappointed by the change. A similar attraction opened at Walt Disney World in April 1973.

The pre-show area included memoribilia from the Walt Disney Archives including awards, letters written to Walt Disney, original animation art, family photos, early merchandise and exact reproductions of Walt's offices at the Burbank Disney Studios. They were reconstructed exactly, using original materials, thanks to the careful documentation and preservation made by Disney archivist Dave Smith in 1970 as well as photographs and blueprints.

The scene outside the window of Walt's formal office was the photographic backdrop that had been used when a replica of Walt's formal office had been built on a soundstage for Walt's introductions to his weekly television show.

The offices were located on the right hand side of the hallway leading to the theater. The working office was removed for display in Walt Disney World's One Man's Dream Attraction in 2001 and remained there until 2015.

A small viewing area on the left hand side featured an audio-animatronics owl discussing Walt's love of animals and his series of True-Life Adventures nature movies and showing video from those films. Display cases along the wall showcased rare treasures.

In the main theater, a twenty-eight minute biographical film of Walt Disney's personal and professional life from his birth to the creation of the Florida Project that included rare stills and film clips was a project that began in June 1969. A staff of more than 200 people at Walt Disney Productions pored over 75 hours of interviews conducted with Walt before his untimely death on December 15, 1966.

Bill Bosche, an artist and producer who worked for Disney for more than thirty years supervised the work. By using excerpts from these interviews, in particular the extensive 1956 ones done with *Saturday Evening Post* writer Pete Martin, Walt Disney posthumously narrated much of his own autobiography.

The film was presented as a virtual photo scrapbook of Walt's life. It was projected through an anamorphic lens which enabled a screen proportion of 2.67 to 1. An edited version was later released briefly on VHS and DVD in a pan-and-scan format.

The exhibit reopened in June 1975 as The Walt Disney Story Featuring Great Moments with Mr. Lincoln with the audio-animatronics Lincoln taking over the stage.

Red Wagon Inn

JULY 1955—JULY 1965

In the 1950s, Swift Foods was one of America's largest producers of prepared meats. They operated the Market House on Main Street, the Plantation Chicken House in Frontierland and the Red Wagon Inn.

It was called the Red Wagon Inn because the icon for Swift Premium Foods at the time was a red, horse-drawn delivery wagon from which the founder started the company.

The restaurant was so prestigious that it even had its own attraction poster and was the only restaurant in Disneyland that served full-course dinners. Breakfast, lunch and dinner were served. The Gold Room and the Green Room on either side of the entrance were for guests.

The menu at the Red Wagon Inn originally offered a varied selection of food, featuring steaks and chops and Swift's quality meats. The restaurant served a lot of sandwiches and some fish, as well. Reportedly, Roy O. Disney was especially fond of the split roast chicken served there.

It included a private dining room called the Hideaway that served alcohol and where Walt Disney could entertain special friends, business partners and Disneyland participants.

General Manager John Mueller remembered that the Red Wagon Inn "featured entrees of chicken pot pie, Swift's premium baked ham, Swiss steak, traditional chef's salad and a fruit plate. We served thousands of meals."

The restaurant featured ornate interior woodwork, chandeliers, stained glass and tile floors that were something of a rarity in a restaurant that offered reasonably priced foods.

The back of the menu provided historical information:

> The Red Wagon Inn on the Plaza in Disneyland offers elegance and glamour reminiscent of famed eating houses of yesterday.

Turn of the century furnishings are authentic mementos of the 1890's. The leaded cut glass entrance doors to the Red Wagon Inn, as well as the stained glass ceiling and back panel of the lobby, were taken from the mansion at No. 20, St. James Park in Los Angeles.

This home was built in 1870 and was one of the luxury homes of the era. Walt Disney purchased this home and removed all the hand carved paneling, newel posts, grand stairway and stained glass that has been used here in the Red Wagon Inn.

Imagineer John Hench recalled:

Swift's Red Wagon Inn is a good example of the authentic theming that Walt wanted. Even the interior had a color scheme of wood that was finished in a yellow-brown that was like tobacco. And naugahyde seat covers that were like chipped beef-a dried blood color. The place was authentic and also kind of depressing.

Swift ended its sponsorship in July 1965 and it was renamed the Plaza Inn and became a buffeteria which cut the time guests spent dining there roughly in half. Walt spent $1.7 million to renovate it and shift to a New Orleans motif. A little red wagon selling corn dogs outside the location today is an homage to the original restaurant.

Circus Fantasy
SPRING: 1986, 1987, 1988

Local publicity for Disneyland's Circus Fantasy event proclaimed:

> Ladies and Gentlemen, Boys and Girls, We direct your attention to Disneyland for Circus Fantasy. It's a circus spectacular too big to fit into three rings, so we're turning the entire Magic Kingdom into the world's biggest Big Top! So run away and join the circus—at Disneyland!

When Michael Eisner became CEO in 1984, he started looking for ways to increase attendance at Disneyland, in particular during the off-seasons. He came up with the concept of having some sort of themed event that would last for several weeks and attract a local audience.

His first promotion was Circus Fantasy that ran from January 25 to March 9 in 1986 and proved so popular that it appeared again in the spring of 1987 and 1988. For the Disney company, it was a revelation that not only was this special event well-received by Disneyland's local guests but it drove a significant increase in attendance and revenue, especially for specially produced merchandise.

It resulted in similar special themed events that followed the same model including State Fair and Blast to the Past that attempted to match its success.

Completely ignoring the individual themed areas of the park, the circus took over Disneyland entirely, The Great Wallenda Duo high wire act going from the Emporium to the Walt Disney Story building; The Centrons motorcycle thrill act that would drive up a wire attached to the Matterhorn; Captain Christopher Munoz "The Human Missile" who was shot out of a cannon over the Rivers of America to a net on the dock of Tom Sawyer Island.

Also John Theron, a swaypole acrobat at the Tomorrowland Terrace; the Diano's Elephants and Castle's Bears at Videopolis as well as a circus themed stage show at Videopolis that was shown several times a day, and circus clowns performing at Clown Alley set up at the Carnation Plaza Gardens.

Former Ringling Bros. Barnum & Bailey Clown College Director Dick Monday and his long time friend Barry "Grandma" Lubin of the Big Apple Circus were among the performers. Clown face painting was held at several different locations.

In addition, twice a day was a colorful Circus On Parade that marched down Main Street, U.S.A. with a pre-parade of the clowns from the Plaza Gardens. For the first year, Mickey started the parade riding on a circus wagon drawn by horses but by the final year, he had is own special float. Minnie rode on top of an elephant.

By 1988, the acts included the Posso Brothers; world-famous high wire aerialists, the Flying Rafaels; Globe of Death which showcased two motorcycles racing around a cage-like iron sphere, barely missing each other in the spot where the *Partners* statue is today; the Winn Family's Astro Sky Cycle; the Wheel of Destiny; Eric Braun and his Performing Dogs; the Trampoline Guys; the circus parade, Clown Alley; and the Circus Fantasy stage show.

State Fair
SEPTEMBER: 1987, 1988

In 1987, to offset the drop in attendance when children went back to school in September, and before the upsurge due to the holiday celebrations, Disney Company CEO Michael Eisner introduced the Disneyland State Fair from September 19 to November 15, 1987. He hoped to capture the same success he had experienced with the Circus Fantasy promotion.

There were Ferris wheels in the hub and one in front of the train station (in 1988 this one was moved to Big Thunder Ranch) and guests could ride them to get a unique view of Disneyland at its apex.

The area in front of It's A Small World had midway games and also a dive tank. Additional carnival booths were in Town Square (with pennants hanging overhead so it looked like a used car lot), the hub, and Big Thunder Ranch.

Games consisted of tossing a ring over something, knocking over bottles, getting a ball in a basket hoop and similar carnival-style amusements that cost anywhere from fifty cents to a dollar for an attempt.

On the stage by the Rivers of America, there was the Lumberjack Timber Carnival with competitions that included tree climbing, log rolling, and ax throwing.

That first year (the event was also there in 1988) Disney gave away state stickers with different Disney characters.

The stickers featured an outline of the state and then a character in front, like Fiddler Pig for Iowa, Donald Duck as a pilgrim for Massachusetts (he was also a lumberjack in Minnesota), Mickey blowing a jazz trumpet in Louisiana (he was also in a straw hat and overalls in Missouri), and Uncle Scrooge throwing money high in air in Nevada among others. Each sticker was about four by two inches and had a peel-off adhesive back.

One of the big attractions was the "State Fair" food offerings, including pies, BBQ turkey legs, and chili.

The "Pigmania" show at Big Thunder Ranch had pig races around a course. Guest sections were assigned a particular pig and called out their special "SUE-EY" pig call to encourage their entry. A race between the Big Bad Wolf and the Three Little Pigs also took place on the course. The wolf never won.

Kirk Wall and his musical group (that would officially become Billy Hill and the Hillbillies in 1992) performed as "The Barley Boys" at Big Thunder Ranch.

As Wall later recalled:

> Our job was to help entertain the crowd and encourage the pigs to run their fastest. Each Barley Brother [Marley, Farley, Charley, etc] would take one of four sections of the audience and teach them a pig 'call' to encourage that pig during the race.

A special State Fair Parade featured John Deere tractors (celebrating their 150th anniversary) and live animals who were blue ribbon winners from county fairs in California. There was even a baby animal beauty contest.

Blast to the Past

SPRING: 1988, 1989

The Blast to the Past Celebration was another attempt by CEO Michael Eisner to increase attendance at Disneyland during the traditional off season of spring through a themed event.

The 1988 season of Blast to the Past event ran from March 18 through June 18. The concept was to capitalize on the nostalgia for the American 1950s and 1960s shown in films like *Grease* and television shows like *Happy Days*.

The Blast to the Past Parade had significant differences each year. For 1988, there were cast members dressed as television show characters like Superman, Lucy & Desi, and Ralph Kramden & Norton. The 1989 version included classic big finned 1950/1960s cars in addition to the appropriately costumed dancers (like roller skating car hops, high school cheerleaders, football players, and gas station attendants). Disney characters were included as well as floats that resembled a gas station, a hair parlor, a rocket ship, and a drive-in theater showing monster movies.

On the weekends, the Main Street Hop performed on Main Street with floats designed like big juke boxes with a malt shop black and white tile floor that held the tables and chairs used by the dancers on the street.

The Carnation Plaza Gardens featured a show entitled Everybody's Rockin' with Goofy. A Beach Party was set up in front of It's A Small World and labeled Surf City with a sand pit in front of the temporary boardwalk-style stage, palm trees and more. Papa Doo Run Run and the Six Ts (Sixties, get it?) were among the performers. Goofy and Donald Duck competed in a surfing contest for the title of the Big Kahuna.

Tomorrowland Terrace was designated the Rainbow Diner that sold burgers and fries along with performances from Big Daddy, the Coasters and Rocko and the Rainbows. In 1989, it became the Soultown Café (showcasing Rhythm and Blues in addition to Doo-wop). Disneyland Sock Hop was held Saturday and Sunday nights at Videopolis along with performances from Herman Hermits, Roy Orbison and the Turtles.

The 1988 season hosted the Super Hooper Duper event, smashing the world's record for the most people hula-hooping at one time in one location—1,527 people gathered in front of Sleeping Beauty Castle. The 1989 season had performer Chubby Checker and 2,248 guests breaking the record for most people doing the twist in one location.

A Blast to the Past Trivia Game had prizes including jukeboxes, 1950s tapes, Wham-O Hula Hoops, Wham-O Frisbees, Fuzzy Dice, Duncan Yo Yos, Jr. Slinkys, Paddle Balls, Large Coca Cola and a chance to win one of five classic 1950s cars.

To participate guests had to fill out the back of their trivia game card and answer three questions correctly and drop it off at one of six entry bins throughout the park.

In the hub, there was a huge jukebox and on the bottom level was a live disc jockey. Local Los Angeles television station KHJ aired a half hour special May 20, 1989, with highlights from the event.

Pooh for President

1968, 1972, 1976, 1980

Winnie the Pooh's first campaign for President began on the night of July 14, 1968, at a special Family Night at the Hollywood Bowl. A host of Disney costumed characters showed up to support Pooh.

The musical entertainment for the evening was provided by the Hollywood Bowl Orchestra and Disneyland's Kids of the Kingdom that featured the release of thousands of red, white, and blue balloons at the finale.

Pooh moved his campaigning to the Tomorrowland Stage at Disneyland to become part of the Kids of the Kingdom show *On Stage U.S.A.* that was performed twice a day. The segment was appropriately called "Winnie the Pooh for President" and sometimes included rotating celebrities like puppeteer Shari Lewis and singer Peggy Lee.

The show was performed during July and August, ending when children went back to school and attendance at Disneyland dropped.

"Pooh in '72" was the campaign slogan for a three day special Disneyland event that ran from October 21 to October 23, 1972. Each day there was a ticker tape parade down Main Street, U.S.A. The Disneyland Band under the direction of Vessey Walker played "Hip-Hip-Pooh-Ray" from *Winnie the Pooh and the Blustery Day.*

Sears was having huge sales of exclusive Disney Winnie the Pooh merchandise so were eager to get on board for the promotion. The Sears stores sold some exclusive "Winnie the Pooh for President" merchandise.

Pooh, Tigger, and Eeyore did meet and greets all day at their National Campaign Headquarters in the Carnation Plaza Gardens.

"Winnie's a Honey of a Candidate" was the campaign slogan for the three day Winnie the Pooh for President event held at

Disneyland October 24-25, 1976. Pooh was touted as "The Children's Pick in '76".

Each day, there was a Main Street "Tigger Tape" Parade down Main Street and Pooh-litical "Fun Raising" Rally in Town Square.

Children up to twelve years old (the Disneyland cut off for when a child became a "junior") were invited to gather in front of the It's a Small World attraction at 1:30 pm. They would be part of the 2:00pm parade through Fantasyland and down Main Street for the big rally in Town Square.

When children exited the park at the end of their day with their family, they could pick up a free "Pooh for President" poster, pin, and coloring kit.

The Fantasyland Theater hosted a free all day showing of Winnie the Pooh cartoons. The Pooh Revue stage show performed three times a day was presented on the Tomorrowland Stage. A special campaign song was written by Larry Groce.

Pooh had one more short shot at running for president in October 1980 at Disneyland but it was much less elaborate than previous attempts. He ran against Captain Hook and guests were encouraged to fill out a ballot thoroughout the day for their favorite candidate.

It is no surprise that when it came to counting the ballots in Town Square, Captain Hook had tried to steal the election but was caught.

Disney Dollars

MAY 1987—MAY 2016

Disney Dollars were referred to as "the money Disney made that makes Disney money."

Jack Lindquist was executive vice president of Marketing and Entertainment for both Disneyland and Walt Disney World in 1987. He got the idea on a flight from Florida to California where he was reading the financial page and realized that the Disney theme parks provided services to more people than lived in some small countries and should have its own currency.

Disney Dollars were first available in a one dollar denomination with a waving Mickey Mouse on the front and Sleeping Beauty Castle on the back, and a five dollar denomination with a proudly posing Goofy on the front and a steamboat on the back. They were illustrated by Creative Service Illustrator Matt Mew and were redeemable for goods or services at Disneyland.

They were first released at Disneyland on May 5, 1987. They were later sold at Walt Disney World beginning October 2, 1987, with the currency being honored at both parks and later at the resort hotels, Disney Stores, Disney Cruise Line and more.

Roughly $60,000 in Disney Dollars were sold just that first day. Buena Park hairdresser Dale Castillo was the first person to purchase a Disney Dollar (actually seventy-five of them) and was presented with a framed plaque signed by Scrooge McDuck.

To discourage counterfeiting, each bill had an individual serial number and was printed on rare, expensive rag cotton stock bearing a subtle watermark. In later years, even more extensive anti-counterfeiting methods were used but there was never an incident of the money being duplicated.

Since September 1987, bills for Disneyland were classified as the "A" series and the ones for Walt Disney World were labeled "D" series. That first year, they were identical at both parks. For the inaugural run, more than two million dollars worth of Disney Dollars was put into circulation, or approximately 870,000 individual bills.

In November 1989, a ten dollar bill was added for both series featuring Minnie Mouse making her the first female to appear on paper currency used in the United States. Over the years, special Disney Dollars were issued including in 2005 a fifty dollar bill to commemorate the 50th anniversary of Disneyland. Every Disney Dollar ever issued included Scrooge McDuck's signature as Treasurer and an image of Tinker Bell on the front side.

Disney claimed that digital purchases and the increased use of gift cards made the expense of fabricating and maintaining these colorful paper gift certificates obsolete. So it was determined that while existing Disney Dollars would continue to be accepted for purchases since they never expire and could be exchanged for the appropriate value of real legal tender, Disney would officially stop producing and selling them May 14, 2016.

New Disney dollars were produced every year since 1987 except 1992, 2004, 2010, 2011, and 2012. The intent was that most people who bought the bills would never redeem them but save them as an inexpensive souvenir and collect the different variations.

Main Street Electrical Parade

JUNE 1972—NOVEMBER 1996

"Ladies and gentlemen, boys and girls...Disneyland proudly presents our spectacular festival pageant of nighttime magic and imagination in thousands of sparkling lights and electro-syntho-magnetic musical sounds—the Main Street Electrical Parade!"

The parade was inspired by The Electrical Water Pageant that included *Baroque Hoedown* as its main musical theme and music produced by a Moog synthesizer. It premiered at Walt Disney World's Seven Seas Lagoon and Bay Lake beginning in October 1971.

Director of Entertainment Bob Jani along with Ron Miziker developed a dry land version for Disneyland the following year with over a half million twinkling lights on floats that were two dimensional flat frames (like the Electrical Water Pageant) on wheels designed by Bill Justice. In addition, cast members attired in lighted costumes accompanied the procession.

When the original contractor could not complete the floats in time, Disneyland itself finished building the floats (as well as using some previously existing parade floats) and installing the lights.

The new parade also used the Baroque Hoedown as it main musical theme interweaved with songs from Disney films produced by a Moog synthesizer that created a somewhat futuristic, other-worldly aspect to the event. Eventually, Don Dorsey used eleven synthesizers to create the soundtrack. Jack Wagner provided the synthesized vocoder voice for the intro and outro to the parade

The original parade floats included the Blue Fairy, a large drum pulled by the Casey Jr. train engine, Cinderella, a Chinese dragon and a circus calliope.

The parade did not operate during 1975 and 1976 as it was temporarily replaced by America on Parade to celebrate the

American Bicentennial. During that break, the MSEP was redesigned with more dimensional floats, a longer running time and a memorable patriotic climax.

The parade units included Tinker Bell, Alice in Wonderland, Cinderella, Peter Pan, Dumbo, Snow White and the Seven Dwarfs, Pinocchio, and Pete's Dragon. Over the years units left or were added including ones for It's A Small World, Briny Deep (*Bedknobs and Broomsticks*), and 1985's *Return to Oz*.

During the summers of 1983 and 1984, the MSEP went dark again and was replaced by Flights of Fantasy but guests eagerly welcomed its return. It continued until 1996 with Disneyland offering guests the opportunity to buy for ten dollars a commemorative display box with an actual light bulb from one of the MSEP floats. The guest demand to catch one last glimpse of the parade was so great that Disneyland had to increase the run by an additional month. The replacement parade, Light Magic, opened in 1997 and was an immediate failure.

Another similar MSEP ran at Walt Disney World's Magic Kingdom from 1977 to 2016 with two major multi-year gaps. In June 1997, the parade was rechristened The Hercules Electrical Parade for one night to promote the animated feature and ran eight blocks in New York City. Versions of the parade later appeared at Disneyland Paris, Tokyo Disneyland, Disney's California Adventure and eventually back at Disneyland for a limited engagement from January to August 2017.

Adventureland

Disneyland opened with only one attraction in Adventureland: the Jungle Cruise.

It underwent significant additions and changes starting in summer 1962 with an enhancement that included Ganesha's temple and nearby ruins as well as Imagineer Marc Davis' humorous elephant bathing pool, the African veldt and the lost safari clinging to a pole with an angry rhino underneath them.

Many things went extinct in Adventureland but primarily shops and food and beverage locations. One of the earliest things that went extinct was that near the front of the Jungle Cruise queue, Walt Disney installed a small pond that was fenced in because it was the home to live baby alligators. Walt wanted guests to see some real animals in addition to the mechanical ones on the attraction.

As Bill "Sully" Sullivan who worked on the attraction in 1955 told me:

> There were four gators and it was fenced with poles and fishnet. They would climb the fishnet and get out. There was a guy who worked with us who was from Florida and he could call them. He could make this sound like their mother and that would help us catch them. Walt got rid of them in the first few months.

Swiss Family Treehouse
NOVEMBER 1962—MARCH 1999

In 1960, Disney released a popular live action adventure film entitled *Swiss Family Robinson,* based on the 1812 novel of the same name. However, Disney made some significant additions to make the story more exciting and amusing.

Directed by Ken Annakin and shot in Tobago (in the Caribbean) and Pinewood Studios (outside London), the film recounts a large Swiss family on their way to New Guinea whose ship is attacked by pirates.

Shipwrecked on an uninhabited island, the father and his two eldest sons salvage material from the ship, including furniture, supplies, and ship parts like the steering wheel and construct a tree house on the island.

Walt Disney felt that children of all ages wanted a tree house of their own and decided using the centerpiece from the film would be a great addition to Adventureland because, at the time there was only one attraction: the Jungle Cruise.

Imagineers thought that it would be a waste of time, space, and money, because guests would never want to climb all the way up only to have to walk all the way back down. When the attraction opened, adult climbers outnumbered kids three to one.

Imagineers studied the gnarled roots of the mammoth Moreton Bay Fig Tree planted in the 1800s by Anaheim horticulturist Tim Carroll to aid in authentically creating details of the Disneyland version. Imagineer Bill Martin was in charge of the ultimate design with input from those people who had worked on the tree for the movie.

The 62 concrete banyan-like roots go down roughly 42 feet and were installed on January 17, 1962. Ten months later at two o'clock p.m. on November 18 (just in time for the extended Christmas hours) the tree was unveiled.

Landscaper Bill Evans, with tongue-firmly-in-cheek, dubbed the original tree "Disneyodendron Semperflorens Grandis" which means "large, ever-blooming Disney tree" and the new version known as Tarzan's Treehouse retains that same designation.

The tree's final cost was $254,900. It utilized six tons of reinforced steel and a 110 cubic yards of concrete. The smaller branches were insired from real Manzanita trees and were adorned with vinyl leaves fiber-glassed onto each branch.

The steel limbs had an 80-foot span and supported a network of a thousand branches with 300,000 handmade vinyl leaves and floral blooms that all had to be attached by hand. The Swiss flag flew from the top of the tree house, which sparked a comment from a confused visitor from Switzerland who told the hosts at the attraction that "the Swiss people do not really live in trees!"

Disney guests had to climb up 68 steps to see all the different rooms and areas like the kitchen, library, Mother and Father's master bedroom, the boys' room and more.

It closed March 8, 1999 to be replaced by Tarzan's Treehouse. A version of the Swiss Family Treehouse still remains untouched at Walt Disney World in Florida, as well as in Japan and France.

Barker Bird

1963

Walt Disney's The Enchanted Tiki Room was a unique experience. No one had ever heard of audio-animatronics. The attraction was owned by Walt Disney himself and not Disneyland so a fee of seventy-five cents was charged for admission. It was also the first completely air-conditioned building at the park in order to keep the computers from overheating.

The theme song of the attraction, "The Tiki, Tiki, Tiki Room," was written by the Sherman Brothers to explain to audiences what they were seeing.

Sculptor Blaine Gibson, who produced the bird shape and the expressive face, recalled:

> Walt didn't want an absolutely realistic parrot, but one with a little bit of cheek on it, something you could get some expression out of.

The four parrot hosts evolved into macaws, amusingly dubbed by the Imagineers as "the MacAudios." The primary host was named José, a Spanish-accented fowl fellow, voiced by Disneyland performer Wally Boag who helped write the script for the attraction.

To help guests understand what the attraction was and to get them to come in to see the show, the audio-animatronics Barker Bird sitting on a bamboo perch by the attraction marquee was installed like a carnival midway barker. It was originally known as the Tiki Room Ballyhoo Parrot but evolved into Juan, the cousin of Jose.

Boag wrote the dialog and voiced the character in a similar comical accent as Jose in several different spiels:

> Amigos, Romans, and Disneylanders! Stop walking while I'm squawking. Walt Disney's Enchanted Tiki Room...is Disney entertainment at its most exciting, best kind. The show is on the inside, not the outside—that would be silly. In the Enchanted Tiki Room you sit down on your feather dusters inside an air-conditioned theater.

The figure appeared in three different versions over the short time it was at the attraction. One figure had red and yellow feathers. Another had red feathers wearing a straw hat and cane, both of which occasionally fell off. The third version was blue and yellow feathers with hat and cane.

The bird had to be removed because large amounts of guests were stopping and clogging the pathway into Adventureland and to the entrance of the attraction itself. The weather also took its toil on the figure. However, thanks to the Barker Bird enough guests saw the attraction so that word-of-mouth made it a success.

For a while, the red and yellow feathered barker bird was in a display case inside The Walt Disney Story in the Opera House on Main Street.

Despite its limited appearance at the park, the Barker Bird became a nostalgic figure for Disney fans. In 2005, Kevin Kidney and Jody Daily created a limited edition Barker Bird figurine sitting on a perch. It was released in an edition of 1500 pieces. They decided to go with the blue and green coloring that became the standard coloring for the character with the 2016 Tsum Tsum Barker Bird, the pin, and the 2018 Funko Pop figure.

Tahitian Terrace
JUNE 1962—APRIL 1993

Tapping into the same love for South Seas culture that inspired the Enchanted Tiki Room, the Tahitian Terrace restaurant simply reformatted and expanded part of the Plaza Pavilion restaurant that already had a Hawaiian themed patio facing toward the Jungle Cruise attraction known as the Pavilion Lanai.

Until the opening of the Blue Bayou restaurant, the Tahitian Terrace was considered the fanciest dining location at Disneyland. It was primarily just open during the summer and during busy seasons for lunch and dinner. The food and entertainment reflected the islands of Polynesia like Tahiti, Samoa, and Hawaii.

It was an outdoor seating area with tables and chairs and a higher level with a roof all facing the stage and served by waiters and waitresses. Unlike other restaurants, there were set times to dine because of the show. It was an approximate thirty minute experience with a live band providing the appropriate Polynesian rhythms.

Originally it was sponsored by Stouffer's but was later taken over by Kikkoman. During construction, Walt Disney felt the tree was too short and suggested cutting it in half and adding a section of concrete in the center. When he told Admiral Joe Fowler he wanted a curtain of water to part and then close again, Fowler immediately replied "Can do!" which earned him his famous nickname.

From the back of the menu:

> Walt Disney has opened wide the portals to an enchanting island world across the blue Pacific...a world of romance, beauty, and exciting entertainment!

> Towering high above you is an amazing tree, a tree that grew (in less than a year) to a height of 35 feet through a secret formula of Walt Disney and his "imagineers"! The branches of this "species

Disney-dendron" are laden with more than 14, 075 hand-grafted leaves and fiery-colored flowers that bloom perpetually. Today this tree is Disneyland's second largest of this rare, unnatural species, exceeded only by the Swiss Family Treehouse.

Nestled beneath the tumbling waterfall is a matchless stage set-ting...a stage whose 'curtain' is a cascade of water, and whose 'footlights' are a leaping flame of fire burning on the water itself! For your summer evening entertainment, the falls magically draw aside...and out from behind the waters, sarong-clad natives appear to perform the swaying rhythms and amazing rituals of the islands...the hypnotic bare-foot fire walk and thrilling fire-knife dance, and the traditional grass-skirted hula of Samoa, Ta-hiti and Hawaii.

Men were brought up from the audience to have a hula lesson. All the guests were given complimentary artificial leis.

At the time, the menu was considered exotic for typical American tastes with Barbecued Pineapple Ribs, Skewered Chicken (with soy sauce), broiled teriyaki steak, coconut shrimp and coconut pineapple ice cream although the highlight for many was the (non-alcholic) Planters Punch Tahitian, a blend of all the exotic fresh fruits of the Islands in a tall frosted cylindrical glass with faux flower memento.

It was replaced by the Aladdin's Oasis dinner show that only lasted two years. The area has recently been revamped in December 2018 as the Tropical Hideaway, a new quick-service lo-cation featuring exotic food offerings.

Aladdin's Oasis
JULY 1993—DECEMBER 2017

Disney wanted to leverage the success of its animated feature film *Aladdin* (1992) so it closed the Tahitian Terrace and changed the architecture of the space into an Arabian bazaar with intricate mosaic detailing and an impressive elaborate entrance archway suggesting something out of the stories of the Arabian Nights.

The master of ceremonies for the Aladdin's Oasis Dinner Show was Kazim, the owner of the establishment and his sidekick Hassan. The show included harem belly dancers, some special effects, a trio of female singers called "The Three Wishes", as well as even a lamp with a costumed character genie who appears. The Genie's voice was snippets of Robin Williams' dialog from the film.

The massive artificial tree remained but the stage now also included the giant Cave of Wonders stone tiger head. Basically, Aladdin ducks into the club attempting to escape the evil Jafar and his henchmen, who soon follow him in; an incognito Princess Jasmine enters to try to find Aladdin but is captured by Jafar, who makes her disappear during an exhibition of his magical powers. Aladdin rescues her with the help of the Genie.

The food served was Middle Eastern delicacies like papadam wafers, mint chutney, fresh fruit with honey-yogurt sauce, shish-kebobs (beef, chicken, or vegetarian), raisin-nut rice pilaf, and tabbouleh among other things. The real specialty was the dessert: a chocolate Aladdin's lamp filled with chocolate mousse and berry topping.

The one hour show was performed eight times daily with segments during the fruit cup appetizer, main course and dessert. It ended in summer 1995 but the location was still used as a table service restaurant on the busiest days.

In 1997, a new show, Aladdin and Jasmine's Story Tale Adventures, a story telling experience featuring characters from the film (actually all of them except Aladdin and Jasmine played by the host Kazoo) interacting with the audience to recap the familiar tale, was performed intermittently over the years but with no food service. It officially closed on 2008 after being on hiatus for some time.

The space was briefly used in the summer of 2008 for the show Indiana Jones and the Stone Tiger (making use of the Cave of Wonders head) as a promotional tie-in with the release of the movie *Indiana Jones and the Kingdom of the Crystal Skull.*

Archaeologist Rachel Flannery was trying to locate a golden idol in the shape of a tiger's head from clues in Indy's journal. Children from the audience assist her in her quest. Indy shows up with the idol but Rachel falls under its spell and Indy must defeat her in a stunt show-like fight.

The area was then primarily used for character meet and greets including Moana besides the Aladdin characters and private parties. A Food to Go program was instituted and tied to special Dining Packages for Fantasmic! and Paint the Night Parade seating. In 2018, the location was demolished to create The Tropical Hideaway.

Big Game Safari Shooting Gallery

JUNE 1962—JANUARY 1982

This attraction had several different names during its existence: Big Game Safari Shooting Game, Safari Shooting Gallery, and Big Game Safari. While the names changed, everything else about the actual attraction remained exactly the same.

It was the largest of the three shooting galleries at Disneyland. It had a larger variety of targets than any other shooting gallery in the United States and the artwork was designed by Imagineer Sam McKim. It had twelve air rifles called "elephant guns".

It was installed in 1962 as part of the additions to Adventureland that would include the Swiss Family Treehouse and new areas of the Jungle Cruise.

The summer 1962 edition of *Vacationland* magazine proclaimed, "If you're a marksman, the new Big Game Safari is for you. While it's based on a time-tested shooting gallery tradition, this jungle hunt is an authentic Disney creation—a one-of-a-kind rapid-fire adventure where you'll shoot at all kinds of jungle animals and birds, each handcrafted for Disneyland."

It was located in the area that previously housed the Cantina between the Guatemalan Weavers shop and the bazaar shopping area. It required a "C" ticket or twenty-five cents for one round. It had a thatched roof and was decorated liberally with bamboo.

Leaning up against the bamboo laced counter, shooters stared across a stretch of water to see the tropical jungle background and hear animal sounds. The proscenium was framed with cut plywood green jungle foliage. The moving targets included lions, tigers, elephants, rhinos, hippos, snakes and other exotic animals as well as tikis and natives. They were traditional chain-driven targets that moved back and forth in front of the African backdrop.

MacGlashan Enterprises had been producing lead shot shooting galleries like this one since 1935 including the one in

Frontierland. Disney bought the company in 1969 and it continued to operate independently.

An attendant would come along with a plastic tube to load each rifle. This gallery used MacGlashan air guns and fired .22 caliber lead pellets that were still powerful and dangerous. They had no gunpowder charge at all, relying on the energy from the compressor alone for propellant.

The lead pellets were so abrasive that they caused severe dings on the targets and the surrounding artwork. As a result, the attraction required new hand painting every night using roughly forty gallons of paint every week. Sometimes it would take up to eight hours to repaint. Eight times a year, the surfaces had to be burned clean and completely repainted.

The repainting required artists because of the intricate patterns like the bark on the trees and the spots on the giraffes that needed the artistic integrity that Walt Disney always demanded.

The pellets would sometimes richochet off the targets, even flying into the guest area behind the shooter. The U.S. government began regulating lead exposure and companies stopped manufacturing the ammunition used at the galleries as demand dwindled. The guns at shooting galleries were later replaced by rifles that utilized infrared beams of lights rather than pellets.

Frontierland

Walt Disney attempted to have Frontierland re-create an authentic frontier experience with lots of real wood, horses and dirt.

However, even though guests enjoyed what Walt provided, they were more comfortable with the Wild West they were familiar with from television and movies and wanted a cleaner, more comfortable experience.

Walt fought as long as he could to keep the horse-related attractions because of his love of horses and the fact they added to the reality of the area. However, they were low capacity, high maintenance, increased liability and high cost. The horses and pack mules were often unpredictable giving the guests an inconsistent experience.

In addition, Disney's version of Davy Crockett waned significantly in popularity after the early years so changes were made to the things that emphasized the iconic frontiersman. Slowly, the land transformed into more of a prosperous mining town with more upscale attractions and restaurants rather than a settlement on the edge of the unexplored frontier.

Even the Marshal's office of Willard Pehall Bounds, named after Walt's father-in-law who had been an actual federal Marshal on the Nez Perce Indian Reservation in Idaho in the 1800s disappeared.

Davy Crockett Frontier Museum / Arcade

JULY 1955—1985

Thanks to the episodes that aired on the Disney weekly television show, Disney's version of frontiersman Davy Crockett was hugely popular and Walt Disney wanted to take advantage of it at the park. He had originally planned the space as a Miniature Museum to showcase his love of miniatures but quickly readjusted it to feature Davy Crockett.

Located just inside the Frontierland stockade entrance, the Davy Crockett Museum was a shop that was decorated like part of the Alamo (where Davy met his demise) with adobe/stucco walls and rough wooden framing. On the walls were some of the framed drawings used in the television program to illustrate the various verses of the famous theme song.

There were many small themed retail areas within the building including a leather shop, BoneKraft run by Richard Swenson featuring items carved from bone, souvenir and clothing areas as well as a display of historic guns showing the evolution of firearms sponsored by the National Rifle Association. It was assembled by author James E. Servern and included actual weapons from the Revolutionary War, Colt pistols from the 1830s and even some "Kentucky" rifles like the kind associated with Crockett. Sam McKim was the designer of the display. In addition, there was also a display of Bowie knives made famous by Jim Bowie.

The museum also had life-sized wax figures of Davy and his friend Georgie Russell as a photo opportunity for guests. They were sculpted by Katherine Stubergh who had created the wax figures for the film *House of Wax* (1953).

They were posed against a backdrop of the Texas plains and guests could borrow a coonskin cap and long rifle to pose with the pair for their official Disneyland photo. They were later relocated in June 1956 to a display room at Fort Wilderness on

Tom Sawyer Island where they were joined by figures of Andrew Jackson and a sentry guard.

In October of 1955, the location was renamed the Davy Crockett Frontier Arcade. The coin operated shooting gallery was called "B'ar Country" where guests could "test their skill with Crocket's Ol' Betsy" with the rifles in a tree stump. It also included six gun pistols for younger guests unable to handle a rifle. Originally, these all shot pellets.

In addition to trees that had owls and squirrels that moved once they were hit, the panorama also included little mechanical grizzly bears that moved back and forth. If a marksman hit the dot on their sides, the bear would rear up and swivel toward the shooter, revealing another dot on its stomach and would remain standing as long as the shooter kept hitting that dot.

The shooting gallery was only a small part of the shop designed like an old frontier building with different sections. The primary space continued to feature a variety of merchandise including clothing, souvenirs, hats (including Davy's famous cookskin cap), items from Mexico, toy guns, rocks and more. It was re-themed as the Pioneer Mercantile, a general merchandise location that opened in 1987.

Mike Fink Keel Boats

DECEMBER 1955—MAY 1997

The last new attraction to be introduced in Disneyland's first year was the Mike Fink Keel Boats on December 25, 1955. ABC had just aired the final two episodes of the Davy Crocket saga: *Davy Crockett's Keelboat Race* (November 16) and *Davy Crockett and the River Pirates* (December 14).

Davy and his friend Georgie Russell poled the keel boat Bertha Mae and their competition was the raucous Mike Fink, the legendary King of the River, and his rowdy crew on the *Gullywhumper*.

Walt realized that these two thirty-eight foot long movie props might be great additions to the Rivers of America and since they were already built, they could be installed quickly to enhance the Frontierland experience.

Both of the keelboats were brought to Disneyland in August 1955 after the filming on the episodes had been completed so that they could be converted with seating benches and two open windows on each side for the guests. With outside and inside seating, each boat held thirty-two guests. Some guests sat on the roof.

The original Bertha Mae was actually redecorated as the *Gullywhumper* and introduced to the park in December. The original *Gullywhumper* required more work and when it made its appearance in May 1956, it was now dubbed the Bertha Mae.

Both boats were built entirely out of wood including pine, cypress, redwood and Douglas fir and lasted for about ten years when they were quietly replaced with new fiberglass boat replicas that were stronger, lighter and had an electrical system. They also now had three windows on each side.

The boats were "free floating" meaning they were not on a guide rail like the *Mark Twain* steamboat so they had more freedom in terms of the trip, often veering toward both banks of the river depending upon the pilot who received extra pay because he was guiding the craft from the back.

They were considered seasonal, only operating on weekends, summer and holidays. Their route was the same as the *Mark Twain* and the canoes. They launched from a dock opposite Tom Sawyer Island near Fowler's Harbor.

On May 17, 1997, the *Gullywhumper* capsized because it was carrying up to forty-nine passengers and became unstable especially with extra guests sitting on top resulting in minor injuries to some of the guests. That incident officially ended the attraction and it never operated again after that day. However, its limited capacity would probably have ended it eventually.

Collector Richard Kraft bought the Bertha Mae for $15,000 from Disney Auctions in December 2001 and starting in 2003, the *Gullywhumper* was used as a prop on the banks of the Rivers of America until it eventually sank to the bottom of the river. In 2010, a new *Gullywhumper* replica was installed in the area where the former burning settler's cabin was located to indicate that Mike Fink had moved in to the refurbished cabin that no longer continually burned.

Indian Village
JULY 1955—OCTOBER 1971

Original concept art had an Indian village with teepees located in front of the stockade entrance to the land but when the park opened in 1955, it originally sat near the border between Adventureland and Frontierland as a collection of teepees on a plot of dirt to resemble an encampment from the nineteenth century.

In 1956, it was moved to the area now occupied by Critter Country across from Tom Sawyer Island and expanded at a reported cost of $100,000. The "villagers" displayed traditions and dances of several different American Indian tribes and an opportunity for guests to meet with Chief Shooting Star (from the Sioux tribe) and have a picture taken.

Disney publicity proclaimed that the "authentic dances from such tribes as the Apache, Navajo, Comanche and Pawnee were performed with the permission of the respective tribal councils and the U.S. Bureau of Indian Affairs". Among the tribes represented were Apache, Shawnee, Winnebago, Hopi, Navajo, Maricopa, Choctaw, Comanche, Pima, Crow, Sioux, and Pawnee.

This new area included a larger, ornate dance circle as well as a dedicated, tiered log bench seating section for guests that surrounded the circle. Usually six authentic tribal dances: the Omaha (called the War Dance by white settlers); the Shield and Spear; the Eagle; the Zuni-Comanche; the Mountain Spirit, and the Friendship (symbol of welcome to visiting tribes) dances were performed summer, weekends, and holidays only. Sometimes the Scout Dance (oldest Indian dance) or the Horse Tail, Buffalo, and others were substituted depending upon what tribes were participating.

The area also had a burial ground, animal hide tepees, a birch bark "long house," spears and other implements as well as a place to demonstrate archery.

The Indian War Canoes guided by Native Americans was introduced that allowed guests to travel the Rivers of America around Tom Sawyer Island. In 1962, the Indian Trading Post was added that sold authentic Indian jewelry, clothing and pottery.

Walt felt that the Indian Village was a celebration of the cultural heritage of American Indians, especially since his wife Lillian grew up in Lapwai, Idaho, on the Nez Perce Indian Reservation. Her father worked for the government as a blacksmith and federal marshal.

As guest interest in "Cowboys and Indians" began to diminish, Walt's passing and with some labor issues arising, the Indian Village was closed in 1971 so the area could be reformatted as Bear Country.

Prominently featured in the Indian Village and in early publicity photos was Eddie Little Sky (also known as Edward Little) from the Sioux tribe who had parts in three dozen feature films and and over sixty television shows.

When Disneyland opened its gates, Eddie and his artist wife Dawn went to work there. She was a narrator hired to explain dances she also performed. Native Americans in the Indian Village also included Laura Rothschild, Bill Wilkerson, Cecilia Blanchard, Foster Hood, the Galaritto twins and many others like Lee High Sky (Shawnee) and Little Arrow (Winnebago).

Pendleton Woolen Mills Dry Goods Store

JULY 1955—APRIL 1990

Between the Davy Crockett Arcade and the Golden Horseshoe Revue was the Pendleton Woolen Mills Dry Goods Store that was sometimes just referred to as the Dry Goods Emporium.

Walt Disney was a fan of the Pendleton product and when the company considered a small retail exhibit in Frontierland, Walt convinced the company to think bigger. At the time, the company wanted to expand its offerings to sweaters, slacks, women's clothing and more so it seemed a good opportunity.

At 2,000 square feet, it was the largest sponsored retail location when Disneyland opened. Chairman of the Board Clarence M. Bishop was listed as the proprietor on the outside of the shop but the actual manager was Harv Johnson. Over its decades in the park, the old-fashioned haberdashery remained virtually unchanged.

Sam McKim did the initial concept art for the exterior of the store that featured a wooden sidewalk often used as porch with guests sitting on the benches. Pendleton was so pleased that they used McKim's artwork on their letterhead for years and in advertisements and on the bags the shop used for merchandise.

The shop sold blankets, sportswear, robes, shirts, jackets, belts, wallets, hats and other Western-themed merchandise. Items sold at the Frontierland store came with a special label, featuring Sleeping Beauty castle and the famous Disneyland lettering as well as the wording: "Frontierland Exhibit".

This particular store set a record for sales of Turnabout reversible skirts in the late 1950s. Visitors were asked what clothing store they patronized in their home town. If that store held an account with Pendleton Mills, fifty percent of the markup on the item was sent to that store.

Walt Disney and his wife, Lillian, were regular patrons of the shop. Lillian bought clothing for their daughters and bolts of yardage. She also picked out the plaid for the Guest Relations hostesses at this store. Walt purchased his blue blazers there that became part of his image.

In the earliest planning stage of Frontierland, the original concept sketch showed a sign for Hyer's Boots, a pioneering cowboy boot maker in Kansas that at one time was the largest manufacturer of handmade boots in America.

One of the reasons Pendleton did not renew its new contract was that the annual rent had increased over twenty times throughout the decades and it was considered too expensive.

C. M. Bishop Jr., president of Pendleton Woolen Mills in Portland, Oregon, said in 1993:

> Over time, Disney decided it was more profitable to take on these operations themselves rather than have them operated independently. One of the reasons we ceased operation at the end of our lease was because of Disney's determination that they could make better use out of the space we were using.

The parting was amicable and even today the company makes special limited edition character blankets for Disney. The location was taken over by the Disney operated Bonanza Outfitters that still sell some Pendleton clothing.

Golden Horseshoe Revue

JULY 1955—OCTOBER 1986

The interior of the Golden Horseshoe Saloon was designed by Imagineer Harper Goff based on his earlier design for an Old West Golden Garter Saloon in the Doris Day film *Calamity Jane* (1953).

The 2,500 square foot interior had a horseshoe shaped balcony, a curtained proscenium stage with private boxes along each side, orchestra pit with a pianist, trumpeter and drummer, a main floor with circular tables and chairs and a long bar covering almost one side of the main floor.

The show originally starred comedian Wally Boag and singers Donald Novis and Judy Marsh but for most of its run the cast was Boag, Fulton Burley and Betty Taylor.

Renie Conley designed the costumes for Slue Foot Sue and the four Can Can dancers. The show was developed by Boag and Novis with contributions from pianist Charles LaVere and lyricist Tom Adair. It was sponsored by Pepsi-Cola from 1955–1982. Eastman Kodak took over sponsorship from 1982–1984.

It was meant to represent a "rootin' tootin'" dance hall revue show with comedy, dancing and singing.

The stage show featured saloon owner Slue Foot Sue and her dance hall girls who welcomed the audience with the song "Hello Everybody". Slue Foot Sue followed this by a flirtatious solo song like "A Lady Has to Mind Her P's and Q's" or "Riverboat Blues" where she wandered through the audience.

Then the Irish Tenor (Novis and later Burley) would do a solo, usually "The Girl on the Cover of the Police Gazette". Then a traveling salesman carrying a carpet bag would come through the audience and get on the stage. Prompted by the pit band yelling out "What have you got there?", the comedian would pull out various items with gag commentary. It was at this point that Boag would do his balloon animal act.

Sue and the Irish tenor would start to perform a song but be interrupted by Pecos Bill (Boag again) and the trio join in singing the Pecos Bill song from Disney's animated featurette. Then the can can dancers take the stage and for the finale the entire cast appear for a final song and bow.

The Guinness Book of World Records lists the show as having the greatest continuous number of theatrical performances with over fifty thousand shows that entertained more than twelve billion audience members. It was Walt Disney's favorite show at the park and where he often took guests to his special box on lower stage left (right side from the audience view).

In 1960, for the athletes at the Winter Olympics in Lake Tahoe, Walt Disney brought up the cast of the Golden Horseshoe Revue to perform. In 1968, the Golden Horseshoe Revue toured for the USO during the Vietnam War. Originally scheduled for Vietnam, they were later sent to Iceland and Greenland.

In 1969, President Richard M. Nixon asked the cast of the Golden Horseshoe Revue to perform at a White House Correspondents Dinner in Washington DC.

Don DeFore's Silver Banjo Restaurant

JULY 1957—MARCH 1962

"The finest barbecue this side of the Mississippi" was served at Don DeFore's Silver Banjo Barbecue restaurant on New Orleans Street in Frontierland. It took over the old location of Casa de Fritos restaurant that had been next to Aunt Jemima's Pancake House but had moved to a more prominent location.

The restaurant was named and operated by actor Don DeFore, who had served as president of the National Academy of Television Arts & Sciences from 1954–1955. He was instrumental in arranging for the Emmy Awards to be broadcast on national TV, which brought him to the attention of Walt Disney and a friendship later developed.

At the time, DeFore was getting acclaim for portraying the next-door neighbor on the popular *Adventures of Ozzie and Harriet* television series and had been one of Walt's guests for the media day opening of Disneyland July 17, 1955. Walt learned that DeFore had helped put himself through college by cooking at his dormitory.

When a space opened up in Frontierland, Walt asked DeFore if he would like to run a restaurant thinking that the actor's celebrity might enhance the park. DeFore and his younger brother Verne eagerly accepted the offer and took a 45-hour business management night class at UCLA Extension to learn how to operate such a business.

The restaurant was cafeteria-style with a cashier at the end of the line and served sandwiches, ribs, chicken, fish, baked beans, cole slaw, and fries among other offerings. It had its own special barbecue sauce based on the famous one served in the chain of Love's barbecue restaurants that the brothers created themselves when the restaurant refused to allow them to use it.

There were a few tables inside, but most were outside with a great view of Tom Sawyer Island in the middle of the Rivers of America and Dixieland jazz music playing in the background. Walt enjoyed sitting outside when he visited the restaurant.

DeFore helped out as a chef while his brother managed the location. The name of the restaurant came from their father's old banjo that he had played to entertain his sons. The restaurant filed as a corporation on March 6, 1957, and opened on June 15. The two brothers' children worked at the restaurant in various capacities including cleaning trays.

DeFore, in his enthusiasm to generate business, actually sparked the ire of Walt and his Disneyland managers by doing stunts like having someone spiel loudly outside, posted large signs, and even put out pots of water with onions so that the smell would entice the guests to his restaurant and increase business.

The kitchen area was too small by Orange County Health Department standards and the storage freezers were outside in a shed, so the restaurant closed in 1962 (not the usually stated 1961) because it could not meet the requirements or afford making the necessary changes. Aunt Jemima Pancake House absorbed the kitchen and dining area and expanded its restaurant.

Aunt Jemima's Pancake House

AUGUST 1955—JULY 1970

The concept for Aunt Jemima had been created by two white men, Charles Rutt and Chris Underwood, founders in 1889 of the Pearl Milling Company. They created America's first ready-mixed pancake flour, and a year later registered the Aunt Jemima trademark for their product. The name Aunt Jemima came from a minstrel show song of the same name whose performer wore the recognizable apron and red bandanna.

Nancy Green, a former slave who had worked as a cook and housekeeper in Chicago, was hired to appear at the Columbian Exposition in 1883 as the character serving pancakes, singing, telling stories and interacting with the crowd and she proved to be a huge hit. She was signed to a lifetime contract. She died in 1923.

The company was sold to Quaker Oats in 1926 who then hired several other performers to portray Aunt Jemima over the decades.

Aylene Lewis made her first public appearance as the character at Disneyland in 1955. She instantly proved to be a charming and charismatic spokeswoman who in her distinctive skirt, shawl, apron and bandanna posed for pictures with guests as she wandered by the tables. She received countless fan letters from people all over the world who had visited.

Located at the intersection of Frontierland and Adventureland, the restaurant was meant to capture a gracious Old South feeling. Outside, landscaper Bill Evans had placed a twenty-two ton Monterey Bay fig tree to provide covering for outside patio dining. Wrought iron balconies graced the upper floors to suggest New Orleans before the Civil War.

Walt Disney was quite fond of Lewis and would often stop by for an early morning breakfast where Lewis insisted on personally serving him and talking with him about the park. She passed away in 1964.

Palmere Jackson sometimes appeared as the character at the park including for the Western Regional qualifying round of the Aunt Jemima Community Pancake Day Races the company sponsored at Disneyland from 1957–1964.

In 1962, the restaurant took over the former Don DeFore's Silver Banjo area that had been next door and expanded and changed its name to Aunt Jemima's Kitchen to match a new restaurant opening by the company in Canada in 1963 called Aunt Jemima's Kitchen that would become a franchise.

The Disneyland location was already credited with serving pancakes to over 1.6 million guests including many dignitaries like Indian Prime Minister Nehru. The restaurant was credited as the originator of the much beloved "Mickey Mouse Pancakes", three pancakes joined together in the familiar silhouette with a face created out of fruit.

Quaker Oats ended its participation at Disneyland in 1967, removed the bandanna from the character (and in 1989 substituted pearl earrings instead) and black actresses were no longer hired to make public appearances.

The Aunt Jemima theme remained at the Disneyland location until 1970 when the restaurant was remodeled and renamed the Magnolia Tree Terrace. In 1971, Oscar Meyer took over the location and renamed the restaurant the River Belle Terrace.

Casa de Fritos

AUGUST 1955—SEPTEMBER 1982

Originally, Casa de Fritos restaurant opened in a small area next door to Aunt Jemima's Pancake House and served "authentic" Mexican food which at the time was considered out-of-the ordinary. Fritos (from the Mexican word for "fried") are a corn chip product of Frito-Lay and were free with every meal.

The restaurant became so popular that it was relocated and opened on July 1, 1957 in the former Marshall's office by the entrance to the Pack Mules. The structure was redone to resemble an old Mexican adobe building making it a perfect backdrop for visits by Zorro as well as a popular strolling Mariachi band.

The opening of Casa de Fritos in Frontierland on August 19,1955 was also the official dedication of New Orleans Street at the park with actress Dorothy Lamour (who was born in New Orleans) and the Frito Kid.

From 1952 to 1967 (when he was replaced by the Frito Bandito), the Frito Kid was the official mascot of Fritos. He was a young blue-eyed boy in a cowboy outfit with a scoop of yellow hair on his forehead (reminiscent of a Fritos corn chip). He appeared in many printed advertisements for the product telling customers to "Meet Me At Disneyland!"

General manager Raoul Casenza oversaw the cooking of the "authentic" Mexican meals. One of its most popular offerings was Frito Chile Pie which was a bag of corn chips sliced open and topped with chili and melted cheese.

Guests could also just get a bag of Fritos from an unusual vending machine designed as a large Frito Kid statue standing just inside the doorway on the way to the counter. He was at the Golden Chips Mine and when guests inserted a nickel, they heard the Frito Kid yelling to his friend, Klondike, deep in the mine who would send a bag of the corn chips down the flume to the guest.

There were a number of different audio tracks so each customer would hear something different. There was even specialty Disneyland merchandise like a mug with the Frito Kid on one side and the word "Disneyland" on the other. The company newsletter has a photo of a smiling Walt putting a nickel in the machine.

Alex Foods of Anaheim supplied the tortillas for the restaurant. One day in 1960 one of the route salesmen saw discarded stale tortillas in the trash and told the cook that he should cut up stale tortillas, fry them, and put a special blend on seasoning on them to transform them into tortilla chips.

A year later, a vice president of Fritos marketing visited Disneyland and saw guests loving these new chips. He asked Alex Foods to mass produce the chips and named the product Doritos ("little golden things") and it debuted nationally in 1966.

The Casa de Fritos evolved into the Casa Mexicana (Lawry's Foods) from October 1, 1982 to 2000. In 2001, the restaurant became the Rancho del Zocalo Restaurante.

Pack Mules

JULY 1955—OCTOBER 1973

Disney executive Van France said:

> Those who dream of the good old days never spent eight hours a day lifting, strapping and unlifting people off of mules. I don't think the (pack mules) made any money. It was a very hard job.

Mules are animals and not ride vehicles. They might stop for no reason or even decide to try to go a different direction. They might let out a loud braying sound or take a nip at the guests or their shoes. The cast members who operated the attraction had to be trained animal handlers, often ex-jockeys.

In the summer, the ten-minute pack-mule excursion into the Disneyland wilderness frontier could be a hot, dusty experience. For the first five years, there was little to see along the trail that looped out and back with perhaps only a glimpse of the stagecoach or Conestoga wagons but mostly pine trees, three small Indian teepees, a small corral with a horse, and a wooden bridge.

For the length of its existence, it was always the highest ticket level partly because of its popularity but also to help offset the high cost of operation. Guests boarded off of a raised wooden platform so that they could easily stride the saddle. While there was no height restriction, there was a weight restriction with the children being placed on the smaller first mules and the heavier adults on the larger ones in the rear.

Operating procedures forbade cast members from asking women their weight. However, they did have to straddle the saddle and could not ride side saddle.

In 1955, the attraction had thirty mules but only fifteen went out at a time in two groups. The trail boss rode a large mule or horse and was followed by seven to eight mules of varying sizes.

The attraction closed briefly in 1956 and reopened in June 1956 as the Rainbow Ridge Pack Mules. Forty-five mules were added at a cost of fifty dollars each. The trail had been lengthened with new ridges and expanded waterways. Riders could now see the Painted Desert with is colored devil mud pots and bleached dinosaur bones.

The Natural Arch Bridge allowed the mules to journey above the new Mine Train which was warned not to toot its whistle at that location for fear of spooking the animals.

The attraction was updated once again in 1960 and renamed Pack Mules Through Nature's Wonderland as the landscape had been transformed to reflect areas from Disney's True Life Adventure films.

A $1.8 million transformation turned the seven acre mule ride into an outdoor scene that included 204 animated animals, the seventy-five foot Cascade Peak with its waterfall flowing into the Rivers of America, and many other additions.

The mule rides ended in 1973. Nature's Wonderland was replaced by Big Thunder Mountain Railroad in 1979. In the town of Big Thunder there is an advertisement: "Pack Mules—Bought, Sold & Rented" paying homage to Frontierland's Mule rides.

Stagecoaches

JULY 1955—SEPTEMBER 1959

Three Concord style stagecoaches (Arizona, California, and Colorado) of the Disneyland Stage Lines were operating on opening day. They had been built at the Disney Studio in Burbank under the supervision of Owen Pope who was in charge of the Pony Farm and maintenance of all harnesses and gear.

The California had a painting of the Santa Barbara Mission on its door. The Arizona had a painting of a butte from Monument Valley. No photos or documentation of the painting on the door of the Colorado seem to exist.

Walt was insistent that the stagecoaches would be period accurate, with many design elements painstakingly fashioned by hand using old-time methods. When Imagineer John Hench objected about the extra time and expense especially on the leather interior straps, Walt assured him that guests would notice if they skimped on the details.

In some ways the trip through the cacti adorned desert, poisoned waterholes, dried bones, desert animals, rock formations and more may have been a little too authentic for some guests as the ride was unexpectedly bouncy and dusty.

Generally six guests rode inside and another six on top. They had to step on the back wheel and with the assistance of the ride operator climbed topside. Another guest could ride "shotgun" next to the driver. It made the coach top heavy which sometimes resulted it in tipping over, especially at a turn in the path.

Disneyland maintained around 200 head of horses, ponies, mules, and burros. The horses and ponies were kept in individual tie stalls, with the mules and burros having their own corrals and lots. Gear was kept clean, polished, and in good repair.

A full-time farrier was on hand (Charles Heumphreus), and barns, stalls, tackrooms, and corrals were kept spic and span. All animals at Disneyland and their quarters were inspected regularly by officers of the SPCA.

Three Mud Wagons were added in 1956 to the existing Disneyland Stage Line and were not named but were simply labeled as coaches "4", "5" and "6". Mud wagons had lower and wider windows on the sides of the coach and were painted bright red with yellow trim and yellow wheels. In addition, all the guests sat pointed forward.

After new scenic landscaping was added to the area, the stagecoaches were renamed the Rainbow Mountain Stage Coaches in 1956. Low guest capacity, high overhead costs and liability safety issues resulted in the stagecoaches and wagons to be eliminated in 1960 with the development of the Mine Train Through Nature's Wonderland.

One of the stagecoaches was sent to the Disney Studios in the 1960s for use as a movie prop. It was used in the California Gold Museum Robbery scene in the film *Return to Witch Mountain* (1978) where it was repainted as "California Overland Stage Line".

For Disneyland's 25th anniversary, one of the original stagecoaches was brought out of retirement and restored for the Family Reunion Parade. It was also on display at the Autry Museum during the park's 40th anniversary.

Yellowstone Coaches & Conestoga Wagons

AUGUST 1955—SEPTEMBER 1959

The announced buckboards never got built for Frontierland but with the need for more capacity, three Yellowstone coaches were introduced along with two Conestoga Wagons roughly a month after the part opened.

Most people just considered the distinctive Yellowstone Coaches as part of the stagecoach fleet but they were very different in several ways.

They were more open and wider and pulled by a team of four horses. They were painted a bright yellow and were based on the Yellowstone Tally Ho touring coaches that operated at that National Park beginning in 1872.

While it had the same undercarriage of the Concord stagecoaches, they were built open-sided with leather seats for all the passengers to look forward and were lighter than the Concord. Several hundred of these coaches operated from 1883–1916.

The Yellowstone coaches also had a tendency to tip over or be subject to the unpredictability of the horses who were often spooked by sudden noises. One team of horses was scared by an unexpected shot of steam from the train passing by in the Painted Desert. The breakaway safety device on the coach malfunctioned and released the front two wheels.

The panicked horses raced along the rest of the trail, dragging the two front wheels behind them. The guests had to walk the rest of the way on the dirt trail back to the loading area.

Two of Disneyland's three Yellowstone Stagecoaches were sent to Walt Disney World in the early 1970s for use around Fort Wilderness Resort taking guests to Pioneer Hall from various "wagon stops" around the campground. Eventually they were replaced by other transportation although one of the coaches was parked on display near Pioneer Hall for several years.

The Yellowstone Coaches and two Conestoga wagons followed the same perimeter loop as the Concord Stagecoaches. Occasionally, the Conestoga wagons encountered a small band of Indians.

Each of the wagons was pulled by a team of two horses. The blue one had a canvas cover that reached halfway down the frame with the words "Westward Ho!" painted on it and the brown one had a similar canvas with "Oregon or Bust!" painted on it. While these were common phrases, it is often assumed that they were to reference the Disney live action films *Westward Ho, The Wagons!* (1956) and *Along the Oregon Trail* (1956).

According to a December 1955 Disneyland newspaper ad:

> It was the Conestoga, not the Covered Wagon that developed the West. The great wagons were first built in the Conestoga Valley of Pennsylvania, with water tight bottoms that permitted safe crossing of rivers.

Actual Conestoga Wagons of the 19th century were pulled by oxen, not horses and pioneer families typically walked alongside their wagons, which were filled with the family's possessions, rather than riding in them like the Disneyland version.

On September 15, 1957, one of the Conestoga Wagons tipped over and sent sixteen passengers to hospitals or first-aid stations for treatments of cuts and bruises but no one was seriously injured.

Cascade Peak

MAY 1960—SEPTEMBER 1998

In 1956, with the addition of new scenery to the Frontierland wilderness, the stagecoach ride became the Rainbow Mountain Stagecoach Ride. It themed in with the new Rainbow Caverns as well as the new storyline that The Rainbow Mountain Mining and Exploration Company had begun activity in the area.

In May 1960, the entire area was redone for the Mine Train Through Nature's Wonderland attraction. Bear Country, Beaver Valley, the Living Desert and electrical mechanical animals were added. In addition, Cascade Peak had been built.

In a *Toledo Blade* newspaper article dated April 6, 1960, Walt Disney explained, that "bighorn mountain sheep will wander atop newly created Cascade Peak, rising 75 feet alongside the Frontierland River with various waterfalls plummeting down its slopes."

Cascade Peak actually looked taller than seven stories because of the little pine trees that had been selected to surround its base. Its main purpose was to block the sight of Beaver Valley and Bear Country from the traffic on the Rivers of America that included the *Mark Twain*, the Sailing Ship *Columbia*, the Mike Fink Keel Boats, and the Indian War Canoes. Its waterfalls also helped aerate the water in the river.

Guests on the watercraft were delighted when their vehicles passed by the photogenic waterfalls that cascaded down the craggy outcroppings of rock. In particular, guests got an up close view of the new landmark by riding on the mine train that went behind the big waterfall and in front of the two smaller ones.

The narration spiel on the attraction intoned:

> If yuh've never gone beneath a waterfall before, then get set, 'cause we're comin' up on Big Thunder, the biggest falls in all these here parts. Yuh don't hafta worry though... unless the wind

changes. Them other two falls they call the Twin Sisters—reckon that's 'cause they're always babblin'.

Of course, the name Big Thunder later inspired the name of the Big Thunder Mountain Railroad that replaced the area in 1979. While Nature's Wonderland was replaced, Cascade Peak remained until 1998. The trees grew taller making the man made mountain appear smaller.

One of the original mine trains and two ore cars were incorporated into a curving length of track near the largest waterfall where it had appeared to have been derailed. In 2016 after many years of sitting abandoned backstage, it was officially donated to the Los Angeles Live Steamers Railroad Museum in Griffith Park where it will be restored and displayed next to Walt Disney's Carolwood barn.

Cascade Peak, of course, was not a real mountain but a building of steel beams and wooden frames built by the same Disney team that had built the Matterhorn a year earlier. Lack of maintenance over the years resulted in severe water damage and termite issues. In addition, work was needed on the faux rock façade. The needed repairs were deemed too expensive and the entire structure became the victim of bulldozers in 1998.

Mine Train

JULY 1956—JANUARY 1977

While the ways to explore the Frontierland wilderness were authentic, they were low capacity and gave guests a very rough ride. In 1956, Walt invested roughly $400,000 for a new attraction that would provide a more comfortable experience as well as handle more visitors.

The little town of Rainbow Ridge with businesses like the Last Chance Saloon and El Dorado Hotel sprung up in the loading area as the fictional Rainbow Mountain Mining and Exploration Company arrived. Guests boarded one of six ore cars (each one holding ten passengers) pulled by a small locomotive on a narrow gauge track to venture on a seven minute frontier excursion.

The four engines were built under the supervision of Roger Broggie and were styled after the industrial steam engines from the turn-of-the-century although there were details like the headlights and wood burner stacks that made them appear even older. They had electric motors and industrial batteries in their tenders. Live narration was provided by either the engineer or the brakeman who was in the last car and heard through individual speakers in each car.

Guests started their trip going through a mine shaft and then passed through rocky cliffs, underneath the Natural Arch Bridge and more including the desert with saguaro cactii that looked somewhat human like the Seven Dwarfs. Guests saw the Devil's Paint Pots with their steaming multi-colored "lava" constantly bubbling before maneuvering between balancing rocks that threatened to fall on the train.

The dramatic conclusion was a trip through the eerie Rainbow Caverns created by Claude Coats where blacklight provided a breathtaking show with the many waterfalls among the stalactites and stalagmites.

In June 1960, Walt Disney spent $1.8 million to expand the area into Nature's Wonderland. The new seven acre wilderness was touted as having 156 types of plant life and over 200 amazing animals, many electric mechanical that would perform simple repetitive movements like a bear scratching its back on a tree.

The expansion had sections to represent Disney's True Life Adventure nature films like *The Living Desert* (1953), *Beaver Valley* (1950), *Olympic Elk* (1951), and *Bear Country* (1953). The attraction had faithful recreations of the forests of Wyoming, the Arizona desert, and the Colorado mountains as backdrops for all the new plants and animals. Cascade Peak now towered seventy five feet in the air with its three waterfalls.

New buildings that emitted humorous sounds were added to the town of Rainbow Ridge. The engine cab and cars were repainted a bright yellow with an additional ore car added to each train and the ride was extended another two minutes..

Guests now went under a big waterfall, over creaking trestle bridges, passed by four spouting geysers and more. Many items from the original attraction were retained including the cactii, the Devil's Paint Pots, and the Rainbow Caverns.

The last ride was on New Year's Day 1977 and the attraction was closed to make room for Big Thunder Mountain Railroad. Several items were retained and used in the new attraction.

Mineral Hall

JULY 1956—DECEMBER 1962

Mineral Hall was a shop operated by the Black Light Corporation of America (a distributor of ultra-violet products in southern California when black light was still a novelty and was owned by Thomas Warren) that was near the exit for the Mine Train in Frontierland and was officially part of the fictional town of Rainbow Ridge (and the famous Rainbow Caverns with its memorable black light finale). In fact, the two story building was meant to resemble the architectural style of the smaller buildings at the attraction.

The location of the shop is now where the Rancho de Zocalo restaurant operates. A second floor window on the front façade of the restaurant is labelled "Mineral Hall".

Walt originally intended Mineral Hall to be a Natural History exhibit similar to one he had seen at the Los Angeles Museum of Science and Industry where a room demonstrated how flourosecent minerals glowed under black lights

However, it evolved into part gift shop and part science exhibit with a series of mineral displays in the back that showed rocks under regular light. Periodically, the U-shaped room would darken and the rocks and minerals would glow eerily under the magic of black light. In addition there were paint and dye samples that did the same. Then the lights would return to normal.

The 1956 park flyer declares: "An all NEW Free Exhibit! Frontierland's Mineral Hall is an exciting display of minerals gloweing in the beauty of black light."

Over the entrance door, a sign stated: "Rainbow Hall of Enchantment." It was one of the first commercial black light stores in the United States. In front was a wooden porch with several wooden chairs.

The shop sold black lights so guests could duplicate the experience at home and fluorescent items including over two dozen rock samples that could be purchased for different prices from ten to fifty cents in a blister pack that had a small bubble with the piece on a red and yellow cardboard card that proclaimed: " From True Life Adventures. Walt Disney's Mineral Land. Rocks and Minerals".

The name of the specimen and its price were at the bottom of the card. Examples included gypsum, granet, moonstone, bloodstone, amazonite, obsidian, turquoise and many more. On the back was information about the particular stone. The shop also sold fluorescent chalk, coloring books and a special Tinker Bell Enchanted Wand that would glow in the dark after being held close to a light bulb for a period of time for only twenty-five cents.

In 1956, Walt Disney purchased a small stump from the Pike Petrified Forest in Colorado that he installed in Frontierland. At the same time, he also purchased one ton of small pieces of petrified stone to sell to guests that was sent directly to Disneyland's Mineral Hall.

Once the shop closed, the nearby Casa de Fritos expanded into the area with some of the space devoted to offices and storage.

New Orleans Square

New Orleans Square was primarily shops and those had a tendency to change frequently in Disneyland. However, other details slowly changed or completely disappeared as well. The Frontierland Train Station now became the New Orleans Square Train Station.

When the area opened in July 1966, guests could hear the chants and ringing bells of a voodoo queen living off a balcony on the backside of the square near the bathrooms and the train station.

It was meant to be the infamous Marie Laveau who practiced voodoo in New Orleans in the 1700s and 1800s. Her portrait could be found in both the Pirates of the Caribbean and Haunted Mansion attractions when they first opened. Her presence disappeared so quietly that few guests even noticed.

One of Walt's favorite locations, the One-of-a-Kind Shop near the Royal Street Veranda closed in May 1996. It sold actual antiques like spinning wheels, Victorian music boxes, vintage dolls, old clocks and furniture. The cost for these items could range in the thousands of dollars. It was replaced in 1998 by Le Gourmet that featured culinary items.

The Disney Gallery
JULY 1987—AUGUST 2007

The Royal Suite (so named because the entrance was on Royal Street) was intended to be a private suite of apartments for Walt Disney and his family just above the Pirates of the Caribbean attraction in New Orleans Square.

With Walt's death in 1966, his older brother Roy felt that the remaining Disney family could not really enjoy the proposed Royal Suite because of their memories of Walt, so the completion was temporarily abandoned.

When the bridge was built in front of Pirates of the Caribbean, construction was taken one step further by adding a pair of ornamental staircases designed by Imagineer Tony Baxter to either side of the balcony of the Royal Suite. The balcony window was transformed into a door, creating a new entrance for the Disney Gallery that opened in 1987.

Original Disney art hung on the walls and display cases housed models of Disneyland attractions. The location also sold artwork, books and items like note cards reproducing some of the art displayed. It also hosted special events like book signings or the release of limited edition prints.

Cast members of the Disney Gallery received approximately forty hours of intense training before their first day in the Gallery. Many of those cast members spent extensive hours of their own time to learn even more so they could share the most accurate information with guests, many of whom became regular visitors.

One of the jobs of the cast members was to monitor the artwork that was exhibited because heat and light could cause severe damage to these treasured items. Lella Smith was responsible for the artwork brought over from Walt Disney Imagineering and ensured that the windows were UV treated, the Gallery was climate controlled and that the environment was generally "artwork friendly."

The first exhibit was "The Art of Disneyland" that ran for almost ten years. Other exhibits included "Tomorrowland: Imagining the Future 1955-1998", "A Brush with Disney: The Art of Herbert Ryman", "100 Mickeys" focusing on the 100 portraits of Mickey Mouse produced by Eric Robison, "Haunted Mansion Holiday" with artwork devoted to the attraction holiday overlay, "A Pirate's Life for Me" showcasing the Pirates of the Caribbean attraction, "Frights, Camera, Action! The Haunted Mansion Goes Hollywood" showcasing the Haunted Mansion attraction and the film, "Disneyland, A Magical Canvas: 50 Artists Celebrate 50 Years" and the final exhibit in 2007 was "Inspired by Disneyland" featuring the art of non-Imagineers like Shag, Kevin Kidney and Maggie Parr that represented their perspectives of Disneyland.

The location was transformed in 2008 into the Disneyland Dream Suite for the special Year of a Million Dreams promotion where guests could win a night's stay in the suites or it could be used for special celebrities. The Disneyland Dream Suite officially closed in 2014.

A smaller version of the gallery relocated to the former bank building on Main Street and later into the interior of the Opera House. It still displays art and hosts rotating exhibits.

The Court of Angels

JULY 1966—SEPTEMBER 2013

The Court des Anges (Court of Angels) opened with New Orleans Square in 1966 and was tucked away around a quiet cul-de-sac. It included a grand curving staircase.

It was officially located at 27 Orleans Street near the train station and featured the same attention to detail including elaborate laced iron balconies in the French Quarter style that were featured throughout the rest of the land.

There were two entrances/exits to this often overlooked location. One was the iron gates that allowed entry from the side near the fountain and the other was a covered short passageway that led directly to the middle of the area.

The location was adorned by a non-working fountain. There was a stone floor. Lush plants, primarily palms, and flowers were in terra cotta pots all throughout the open-aired courtyard. Up above light strands lit up the area at night along with lanterns on the ground and walls. At the top of a building by the staircase was flown the Louisiana state flag.

Above the staircase was a sign with the words "Court des Anges" along with a plaque on the wall that states: "Musique Des Anges Music Lessons Vocal Instructions Mme. Sally McWhirter Instructor" that was installed July 1998.

The plaque was placed there in remembrance of Sally McWhirter. She began her Disney career in the Disney Stores in Indiana. She was promoted to District Manager before coming to work at Disneyland. She was named director of Disneyland store operations in 1995 and continued working until her passing in December 1997 at the age of 40 from a virus after battling cancer. Sally loved to sing in her church choir which is why on the plaque music is mentioned. Halfway up the staircase there is a statue of a boy angel holding a woodwind instrument flanked by oil burning lamps.

The Court of Angels was a popular "hidden" location for Disneyland fans who often came back every year to take a photo on the staircase and with benches being a welcome respite to sit and relax from the chaos in the rest of the park. It was also occasionally used for character meet and greets as well as engagements.

With the expansion of the private Club 33 restaurant, there was a need for more space as well as an increased capacity elevator for guests with disabilities to get to the location. The new elevator is where the old bathrooms once were.

The irons gates that close off the Court were preserved with the exception of a new large stained glass door added to block off the area to the public. The area is now a staging area for the restaurant with tables and chairs. In addition, trees were trimmed lower to allow a better view of Fantasmic! The stairway remained the same but is now only accessible to members of Club 33 and their guests since it leads directly into the restaurant.

Pirates Arcade Museum

FEBRUARY 1967—1980

The official entrance was on Royal Street but most guests found the side entrance immediately as they exited the Pirates of the Caribbean attraction.

It was turned into the merchandise shop Pieces of Eight in 1980 and all the arcade games were eliminated. In their place was more pirate merchandise. It later became more themed to merchandise from the *Pirates of the Caribbean* movie franchise.

It was much more of an arcade than a museum with arcade games that included Cap'n Black, Captain Hook, Freebooter Shooter (shooting at drunken pirates teetering on kegs like the final scene in the Pirates attraction), Pirate Shoot, Th' Devil T' Pay, Blackbeard and Candle Snuff. The games were all basically different variations on target shooting but with distinctive pirate imagery.

The souvenir guidebook stated: "Pirate games for a doubloon or a handful of coins." Actually all games were just a dime.

The location was decorated with pirate themed decorations including treasure maps, Jolly Roger flags, portraits depicting infamous pirates, fishing nets, rum jugs, vintage lanterns, "treasure" and miniature ships. In the background, a lively instrumental version of the song "A Pirate's Life for Me" filled the air.

It also included a vending machine with two sets of six postcards each featuring Marc Davis' concept art for the Pirates attraction and a pieces of eight coin stamping machine. Imagineer Sam McKim was put in charge of designing the location.

McKim told Leon and Jack Janzen:

> I had come up with twenty or thirty possible ideas to turn existing machines into pirate situations. Dick Nunis and I eventually did sixteen machines for that arcade. Walt never saw the finished area but he saw a mock-up I had done and all of the drawings.

I also had a sample shooting game that had been veneered with wood and rope trim and period weapons that Walt saw. I went out and bought the original "piece of eight" coin that they then reproduced for the stamping machine by the door. That was my baby. I paid fifty dollars for that coin and it would be worth a lot more now. It was authentic, actually brought up from a sunken Spanish galleon in the Dutch East Indies.

It eventually turned up missing from the safe in the finance department. We also rented a number of antique coins for WED to copy. We made castings and reproduced them to use in the foreground of Fortune Red and the other machines in the arcade. I designed the Fortune Red fortune telling machine.

Originally the fortune telling machine was to be a full-sized buccaneer with a missing leg and a parrot resembling Long John Silver from Disney's live action film *Treasure Island*. Eventually, it was easier to make him like Main Street, U.S.A.'s Esmeralda fortune telling machine. So the red-bearded pirate from the waist up pointed at his treasure map and dispensed arcade cards with a fortune in pirate lingo on one side and historical information on the other.

Holidayland

JUNE 1957—SEPTEMBER 1961

Holidayland was a nine acre picnic-type area designed as a space that could be rented by corporations or outside groups for an outdoor event. It could accommodate up to 7,000 people and was located just behind where New Orleans Square is today.

It had playgrounds with swings, slides, and more. It also featured baseball fields, volleyball nets, horseshoe tossing pits and picnic tables, along with a raised stage for entertainment under "the world's largest candy-striped circus tent" that had been used for the ill-fated Mickey Mouse Club Circus in 1955.

Holidayland, located outside the perimeter berm, also had a separate gated entrance into Disneyland through Frontierland. The area resembled a city park. Basically, the show building for Pirates of the Caribbean is where the baseball fields were and the Haunted Mansion show building is where the circus tent stage area was.

The Holidayland Picnic Committee included Bill Stewart, Van France, Howie Vineyard, Cap Blackburn, Bob Carbonnel, Tommy Scheid, Bob Reilly, Barbara Bray, Marty Sklar, Jack Sayers, Dick Stovall, Tommy Walker, Ray Webster, Earl Shelton, and Larry Tryon.

Primarily it was Milt Albright who was put in charge as overall manager and he tried his best to make it a success but many factors undercut his efforts including the fact that it was temptingly close to Disneyland but did not allow the guests into the park without a special admission ticket.

The first event held in Holidayland was the Los Angeles Elk's Lodge No. 99 Picnic on Sunday, June 16, 1957, for 5,000 members and their families. The event included a performance by the Disneyland Band and a 30-minute performance by the Mouseketeers. Smaller sized groups had to settle for their own entertainment, like sack races and bingo games.

Since it was technically not in Disneyland, it had concession stands that included the sale of beer. Guests could purchase a picnic basket lunch prepared by the Red Wagon Inn that included all the beer a person could drink.

"Walt thought beer was a basic part of a picnic," said Jack Taylor, the first operations supervisor at Holidayland. "But he never wanted it inside Disneyland."

Admission to Holidayland did not include admission into Disneyland, although some people tried to sneak in across the railroad tracks. Admission tickets and a reduced price ticket book were offered to try to alleviate that activity but were ineffective.

As drunks from the area stumbled their way into the park, the sale of beer was curtailed. As Walt predicted, too much alcohol transformed some people into howling nuisances.

In the beginning there were only very small restrooms and no nighttime lighting. Walt soon introduced portable restrooms, and eventually built permanent restrooms just before the area closed forever in fall 1961. The previous year strong winds had literally torn the circus tent to shreds and it was decided not to invest in repairs.

By the way, it was called Holidayland because the promotional information for the area declared it to be "A recreational park where every day's a holiday."

Critter Country

Originally the area had been an extension of Frontierland and featured the Indian Village. The huge popularity of the Country Bear Jamboree attraction in Walt Disney World prompted Disneyland to create an entire new land called Bear Country that would showcase that attraction. It spent roughly eight million dollars on the four acre spot.

Bear Country opened in 1972 with the main attraction being the Country Bear Jamboree. The Indian Trading Post remained as did the canoes but now they were themed to Davy Crockett. The Hungry Bear Restaurant appeared. The Golden Bear Lodge and Mile Long Bar also were added along with Ursus H. Bear's Wilderness Outpost.

With the upcoming opening of the Splash Mountain attraction, the entire land was re-themed in 1988 as Critter Country since there were more animals than just bears that were living in this quiet, woodsy location although the bruins still had a prominent presence.

The Mile Long Bar and Teddi Barra's Swingin' Arcade became the Pooh Corner shop that sported a sign stating "Critter Country est. 1889" referencing the opening of Critter Country in 1989. The Indian Trading Post became the Briar Patch store.

Country Bear Jamboree
MARCH 1972—SEPTEMBER 2001

In a beautifully ornate proscenium theater in Bear Country (later Critter Country), a variety of audio-animatronics bears and a handful of other animals like a raccoon perform a series of musical numbers with a country and western theme on multiple different stages, just like an old fashioned knee-slapping hoe-down at the Grand Ol' Opry...but with lots more fur.

The concept art for this lively show was some of the last artwork ever seen by Walt Disney himself and it gave him a good laugh shortly before his untimely passing. Designed by Imagineer Marc Davis, the Country Bear Jamboree was originally intended to be an indoor attraction at the Bear Band Restaurant in Disney's planned Mineral King Ski Resort to be built in California in the 1960s.

As Imagineer Wathel Rogers recalled:

> After the Mineral King contract had been signed, Walt had an idea for entertainment after people had been skiing. Walt said, "What we are going to do is have a bear band and have them perform two or three programs of entertainment. We'll say that the bears had come out of the sequoias and we trained them to be entertainers."

The Mineral King project fell through, and the show premiered opening day at the Magic Kingdom in Florida, where it received so much positive guest feedback that a replica was built in Disneyland in California with two theaters (both Disneyland theaters replaced in 2003 by that British bruin, Winnie the Pooh and his attraction). It was the first new ticketed attraction at Disneyland since the Haunted Mansion in 1969.

The back story for the attraction was that Ursus Bear, after a restful hibernation, rounded up his musically inclined kinfolk and friends to put on a down-home celebration.

Over the years, a variety of different shows with different costuming and songs have rotated through including a Christmas Special show (introduced in 1984) and the Vacation Hoedown (introduced in 1986) that continued to be the show until 2001.

Performances were by master of ceremonies Henry (and his raccoon hat Sammy), Gomer the piano player, The Five Bear Rugs (Zeke, Fred, Ted, Zeb, and Tennessee with Zeb's non speaking son Oscar and his teddy bear sitting on the edge of the stage), Wendell who plays the mandolin, Liver Lips McGrowl, Trixie, Terrence, The Sun Bonnets (Bunny, Bubbles and Beulah), Ernest the fiddle player, the "swinging" Teddi Barra and the unforgettable Big Albert. The never seen Rufus was the stagehand who ran the projection booth among other chores. On the adjacent wall, the talking heads of Buff the bison, Max the deer and Melvin the bull moose often joined in the festivities.

Some of the songs in the original show were "Mama, Don't Whip Little Buford," "All the Guys that Turn Me on Turn Me Down," "Blood on the Saddle," and "The Ballad of Davy Crockett." The Vacation Hoedown featured "On the Road Again," California Bears' "Thank God I'm a Country Bear," "The Great Outdoors," and "Rocky Top."

Rufus the Bear

JULY 1972—SEPTEMBER 2001

To enhance the pathway between the Haunted Mansion and the entrance to the newly opened Bear Country, the Imagineers installed a cave on the mountainside just above eye level. The cave was identified as being the home of Rufus the bear who was in constant hibernation.

To the delight of many guests, a distinctive snore constantly emanated from the cave opening.

The snore was originally recorded sometime in the mid-1930s, probably by storyman and voice artist Pinto Colvig, to be used for the dwarf Sleepy in *Snow White and the Seven Dwarfs* (1937). At some point perhaps because it might have been intended for the deleted bed building sequence, it ended up never being included which was not an uncommon situation for things recorded for the early Disney animated feature cartoons.

It was discovered in the Disney Studios sound library decades later and incorporated into an El Dorado Hotel second floor room in Frontierland's mining town of Rainbow Ridge façade. Rainbow Ridge first appeared as part of the exterior of the Rainbow Caverns Mine Train as early as 1956 where workers from the Rainbow Mountain Mining and Exploration Company spent their time.

In 1979, the town was officially renamed Big Thunder as seen on a population sign to theme with the new attraction Big Thunder Mountain Railroad but the snore remained.

Then the snore was moved to the opening of Rufus' cave. For awhile in Bear Country, the exterior of the men's restroom in the area was themed as Rufus' dressing room. (The female restroom was themed to Trixie.)

The famous sleeping bear was not originally part of the Country Bear Jamboree but was incorporated into the show with the holiday overlay Country Bear Christmas Special that debuted in 1984. Rufus was now the sleepy, lone stage hand in charge of fixing lights, running projections and changing backdrops.

He is constantly admonished by Zeke, Wendell or Henry for not having something working. Poor Rufus who is never seen is often heard to be out of breath as he struggles to run to different locations to fix things, sometimes resulting in something crashing to the floor in the booth behind the audience or a sudden electrical jolt.

He generally just speaks in surprised grunts. He was also incorporated into the Country Bear Vacation Hoedown show that premiered in February 1986 in a similar role.

With the introduction of Splash Mountain in 1989, Rufus' cave was moved up the mountain by the ride track just before the first waterfall and his famous snore was still evident.

Once the Country Bears disappeared in 2001, the Imagineers realized that most guests would not have any idea who Rufus was so that it made more sense to change the sign to indicate that it was the home of Brer Bear who was featured so prominently in the attraction. The exterior was redone to feature items belonging to that snoring bruin and Rufus, like the rest of the Country Bears, faded into obscurity at Disneyland.

Indian War Canoes /
Davy Crockett Explorer Canoes

JULY 1956—???

The Disneyland canoes were the only attraction to appear in three different lands without moving: Frontierland, Bear Country and Critter Country.

They primarily operated only during the summer, weekends and holidays since they required two cast members (one front and one back) for each canoe making it expensive to operate in relationship to the limited capacity. The attraction did not operate on rainy days and only ran during daylight hours.

When the area they were located in Frontierland was renamed Bear Country, in May 1971, they became the more politically appropriately named Davy Crockett Explorer Canoes and remained so when the land was renamed Critter Country.

The Disneyland website states:

> Named after the legendary frontiersman, Davy Crockett's Explorer Canoes transport you back to a time before highways, when water was the fastest mode of transportation and an exciting new discovery was around every river bend.

When they were named the Indian War Canoes, only Native Americans were the guides on each canoe. When it became the Davy Crockett Explorer canoes, it became any well-bodied young men. In June 1995, women finally took up the oars to paddle around the Rivers of America.

The original thirty foot long canoes were built by Old Town Canoe Company of Old Town, Maine. Those first canoes were made of wood and equipped with an air filled chamber that ran the length of the canoe for stability.

Today, each 35-foot-long fiberglass canoe holds eighteen guests, two per row. Each canoe still has two guides dressed as frontier explorers at the bow and stern. Guests are given a short lesson on how to paddle but the primary work, especially guiding the canoe since it is not on a track but free floating and does not have a motor, is done by the two cast members.

Disembarking from a small dock near the Hungry Bear Restaurant, the guests journey around Tom Sawyer Island, often encountering other river traffic like the *Mark Twain* steamboat which has the right of way. The attraction offers a unique perspective and an up close look at things seen from the bigger ships.

In 1963, Ray Van De Warker, foreman of the Indian War Canoes noticed a guest canoe filled with athletes charging around the Rivers of America. Discussing this with Jungle Cruise *foreman* Bob Penfield about how fast each of their teams could get around the river sparked the beginning of the cast member canoe races.

Disneyland employees sometime compete in these canoe races early in the morning before the park opens. They also hold competitions during the summer season, awarding trophies to teams that are the fastest or have the most improved times.

They were similar canoe attractions at Florida's Magic Kingdom, Tokyo Disneyland and Disneyland Paris but they all closed by 1994. The Disneyland canoes have disappeared for significant stretches of time over the decades and have been a constant source for rumors of permanent removal which is why they are included in this book.

Fantasyland

While Fantasyland seems timeless, the entire land went through a major renovation in 1983.

It was dubbed "New Fantasyland" when it opened May 25, 1983, and shifted the exterior architecture from that of a medieval fair to an old European village from the time of the classic fairy tales.

Many attractions disappeared or significantly shifted location and even some new attractions were added. Imagineer Tony Baxter primarily supervised these changes in the belief that Walt Disney was hampered by budgets when the park first opened so could not complete his original vision for the area. He was inspired by the architecture of the miniatures in the Storybook Land Canal Boats attraction.

King Arthur's Carrousel, the Mad Hatter Tea Cups and Dumbo were all relocated. Mr. Toad's Wild Ride and Peter Pan's Flight were upgraded. Pinocchio's Daring Journey was added as was the Village Inn (now known as the Village Haus). The wicked queen now peered out of the curtains above the Snow White attraction.

Today, all of these changes are now considered the "traditional" Fantasyland. Baxter recalled on opening day hearing a lady say, "You know, it is like it was always here."

Mickey Mouse Club Theater / Fantasyland Theater

AUGUST 1955—DECEMBER 1981

The theater was located in Fantasyland approximately where Pinocchio's Daring Journey attraction is today. It was air-conditioned and seated 400 guests.

Disney producer Harry Tytle was in charge and put together special half hour programs of Disney shorts that continually re-ran. In those early days, the theater was closed during slack periods and opened only during the weekends and summer when the crowds were the heaviest.

The souvenir book from the time only claimed "30-minute cartoons running continuously from 11 a.m. to closing" and it would have cost a "B" ticket to attend.

Tytle remembered:

> Walt proposed a show, utilizing 3-D cartoon shorts which we made years before, which would run for twenty minutes. This meant a new show every half hour, with ten minutes between screenings.
>
> He had director Bill Beaudine, direct a special live-action opening, utilizing the Mouseketeers. We were to use between 15,000-20,000 3-D glasses per week. As a result of the new show, attendance soared.

3-D Jamboree at Disneyland ended up being closer to 26 minutes and premiered at the theater around June 16, 1956 and ran until sometime in 1959.

The live action was directed by William Beaudine and written by Larry Clemmons (with the live action 3-D camera supplied by Arch Oboler known for one of the first live action 3-D films, *Bwana Devil*).

3-D Jamboree featured the only known color-film footage of the original Mouseketeers in 3-D. Annette, dressed as a ballerina, appeared to soar toward the audience on a swing, while Jimmy Dodd seemed to douse the audience with a bucket of water. Lonnie Burr had an old-fashioned camera that had a clown head that popped out of the lens toward the audience and Roy Williams participated in a comical pie fight.

The short live action framing sequence included two cartoons that the Disney Studio had made in 3-D. *Adventures in Music: Melody* released May 23, 1953, had Professor Owl instructing his classroom of distinctive bird students about the musical concept of melody. *Working for Peanuts* released November 11, 1953 featured Chip and Dale stealing peanuts from Dolores the Elephant, but zoo keeper Donald Duck stepping into the battle.

Both *Melody* and *Peanuts* were also photographed as regular flat 2-D animated cartoons, and that is how most Disney fans have seen them on television and video over the years.

When the show closed in 1959, it took until 1982 for the Disney theme parks to showcase another 3-D film experience. That's when Magic Journeys opened as part of the Journey Into Imagination pavilion at Epcot.

The theater was rechristened the "Fantasyland Theater" in 1964 and after that 3-D show continued to run a collection of regular 2-D Disney short cartoons until it closed in 1981. During its existence, the theater was also used for meetings and training sessions when not in operation for the guests.

Welch's Grape Juice Stand

JULY 1955—1981

From 1955 to 1958 Welch's was one of the sponsors for the syndicated original *Mickey Mouse Club* television show. They even had Disney artist Tom Oreb who worked for Disney's secret commercial division known as Hurrell Productions create a crafty fox named Foxy Loxy and his adversaries (two Indians named Pow'n'Wow).

The characters were used for animated commercials and print advertising for Welch's grape jelly in the mid-1950s. The fox was always trying to steal grapes and the Indians convinced him that getting Welch's grape juice or jelly was better.

"Disneyland's headquarters for healthful refreshment", as it was advertised, was located on the right hand side of the Mickey Mouse Theater (later changed to Fantasyland Theater in 1964) in the spot that now houses Pinocchio's Daring Journey that opened as part of the New Fantasyland in 1983.

"You'll meet lots of old and good friends in Fantasyland. One of the best, especially when you're thirsty –is cool, delicious Welch's Grape Juice," claimed a 1955 advertisement.

Bob Penfield said in 2015:

> I was supposed to work at Peter Pan on [July 17, 1955], but it wasn't running, so I got moved to the carousel. It was very hot and [there were] no drinking fountains working in Fantasyland at the time. So every time I got a break from work, I went over to the Welch's Grape Juice Stand.

Above the counter was a huge curved purple, lattice-like archway with the word "Welch's" in blue decorated by lots and lots of green plastic grapes. Underneath were three round glass containers containing grape juice. Even the trash can outside was bright purple with the word "Welch's" on it.

Medieval shield signs above the corner entrance featured the word "Welch's" with a bunch of grapes underneath.

Across the entire back was a huge mural showing the centaurs, centaurettes, a unicorn, a faun, and several winged cherubs from Disney's animated film *Fantasia* marching to the right. The lead centaur and centaurette carried baskets of purple grapes so the other characters were following them to sample the treat although many of them were also carrying bunches of grapes in their hands.

The mural was painted by artist Eyvind Earle who was art directing the distinctive style of Disney's animated feature *Sleeping Beauty* (1959) at the time. Actually Earle worked with Frank Armitage on it as they teamed to do other early Disneyland murals like for the old Castle Arts and Crafts Shop.

A re-creation of the mural is at the Bacchus Lounge, a small bar just off of the main lobby at the Shanghai Disneyland Hotel. Bacchus was the god of wine which came from grapes and spent most of the animated sequence in a state of inebriation. The artwork depicting the character is based on the film.

Besides selling grape juice (purple, red and white) served in little plastic purple cups that looked like a bunch of grapes, the stand also sold bags of chips for thirty-five cents, frozen grape juice bars and grape popsicles.

Midget Autopia
APRIL 1957—APRIL 1966

The Autopia attraction in Tomorrowland was hugely popular when it opened in 1955, resulting in Walt opening the similar Junior Autopia in Fantasyland in 1956 to try to handle the demand.

To accommodate younger children, the seats were higher, had extended gas pedals, and a guide track, but other than those modifications and a shorter track layout, it was basically the same experience.

Also in Fantasyland, near the Storybook Land Canal Boats in 1957, Walt introduced the Midget Autopia for the smallest of Disneyland's guests who still might not be able to reach the height limit or steer properly or operate the gas pedal. Today, the word "midget" is avoided, but in 1957 it just meant "small".

In a 1956 memo, Walt had proposed the creation of a Mousekatopia area in Disneyland devoted to the youngest children that would include a helicopter ride, boat ride and a car ride that were fairly standard at many amusement venues. He later changed his mind about that expansion because the rides would separate families, but he did go ahead with the smaller Autopia because the demand was so great and he didn't want even the smallest children to be disappointed.

Unlike other Disneyland attractions, no adults were allowed on the Midget Autopia. It was more like a cartoon experience than a miniaturized driving opportunity for two people. It was an off-the-shelf amusement park ride that was purchased and enhanced by Arrow Development who had worked on some of the Fantasyland attractions. The cars included headlights from a '56 Pontiac and hood ornaments from a '57 Chevrolet.

Unlike the larger cars that ran on gas, these smaller, rounder cars ran on electricity on a bus bar track much like the popular dark rides so the drivers could not accelerate or brake like the other versions. The route was not the freeway but a gentle, winding, rural road. The journey went over a small hill, through a short tunnel and a yellow garage barn where the doors swung open at almost the last minute.

Imagineer Bob Gurr told me in 1997:

> They were just simple four-wheel dark ride cars. Arrow had been building and selling them to other parks for years, and these were not Autopia cars in the sense that you could drive or control them. The Midget Autopia was a 'kiddie' ride with the same technology used on almost all dark rides.

There were two steering wheels so each passenger had access to one, but the wheels were unconnected to anything so spun freely. The attraction was generally just open during the peak park hours during summer, holidays and weekends.

After the attraction was dismantled in 1966, it was donated by Walt Disney himself to his hometown of Marceline, Missouri, where it was installed by Admiral Joe Fowler who also handled the training for the ride. It operated in the Walt Disney Municipal Park for eleven years until maintenance and insurance became major challenges and it was closed.

Chicken of the Sea Pirate Ship Restaurant
AUGUST 1955—AUGUST 1982

Van Camp Seafood used the phrase "Chicken of the Sea" to describe the taste of its tuna as being mild and having a white color just like chicken and was so successful that soon it also became the company name.

Imagineer Bruce Bushman came up with the original drawings for the eighty-foot tall wooden ship, intending it to be an exaggerated version of Captain Hook's vessel from the Disney animated feature *Peter Pan* (1953). Its striking black hull and massive sails made this Fantasyland icon very impressive as it sat in a small pond of water.

Instead of being an accurately scaled sailing ship, it was meant to be more fanciful with its oversized crow's nest on four tall masts and the red and white striped canvas sails to fit in with Fantasyland. The entire ship made of Douglas fir was built backstage at the Main Street Opera house mill and then lifted by a construction crane to be put in Fantasyland.

The mermaid figurehead (meant to resemble the mascot of the food brand) on the bow of the ship was sculpted by Chris Mueller from designs by Imagineer Marc Davis, his first work for Disneyland. Mueller was also responsible for the twenty foot wide fantail for the ship. The restaurant opened August 29, 1955.

Customers entered by crossing a pier-like bridge of planks. In the earliest days, a real peg-legged pirate named Captain Guy (a Korean War veteran who had lost his leg during that conflict) with an eye patch and a live talking parrot named Paco who liked to bite things interacted with guests.

The specialty served at the counter in the hull was tuna sandwiches (along with tuna burgers, tuna pies, and tuna salad) which guests could take upstairs to the main deck or go to one of the canvas awning shaded tables outside at the port side of the ship.

The upper deck gave an unobstructed view of all of Fantasyland at the time. A beautifully sculpted and tropically exotic Skull Rock Lagoon was added in 1960. Skull Rock with its waterfalls was thirty feet tall.

In 1969, ownership passed to Disneyland and it was officially renamed Captain Hook's Galley.

With renovations for a New Fantasyland in 1983, an attempt was made to relocate the ship but extensive damage to the lower hull and concrete that had replaced rotting wood prevented that from happening and the ship was demolished. The Dumbo attraction is now located where the ship once was harbored and the watery rock work near the queue is all that is left of Skull Rock Lagoon.

However, some of the details from the ship were relocated to the newly rehabbed Peter Pan's Flight attraction. The ship's wheel that Peter steers is from the famous vessel along with some of the rigging, bailing pins, and lanterns that were also salvaged. Disneyland Paris re-created Captain Hook's ship counter service restaurant and nearby Skull Rock in its Adventureland.

Skull Rock Cove

DECEMBER 1960—AUGUST 1982

One of the most dramatic scenes in Disney's animated feature *Peter Pan* (1953) takes place at Skull Rock in Neverland Lagoon. Captain Hook and Mr. Smee take the Indian princess Tiger Lily to the location and threaten to drown her at high tide if she does not reveal the whereabouts of Peter Pan. Fortunately, Pan rescues her just in the nick of time after a battle with the villainous Hook.

Skull Rock does not exist in the original James Barrie novel but was the creation of the Disney artists for the film's story.

For the first five years of the park, the Chicken of the Sea Pirate Ship Restaurant that was meant to represent Captain Hook's infamous ship was anchored in a shallow pool. The surrounding area was devoid of any landscaping. It looked unfinished next to some of the other attractions. It seemed natural to put it into an appropriate setting from the film.

In late 1960, Skull Rock Cove was added to the area and included sandy beaches, an outdoor dining area with tables and chairs made of the ship's kegs, palm trees and a pathway leading to volcanic rock outcropping.

Rockwork stood thirty feet tall and curved around the northeastern shore of the lagoon. The massive rock that resembled a skull was designed by Imagineer Ken Anderson. The new addition not only added to the atmosphere of the pirate ship but screened the Casey Jr. train from view and helped the transition to the rocks that surrounded Monstro the whale just around the corner.

From the skull's open mouth, a waterfall poured out over the craggy lower teeth. Several smaller waterfalls at various heights cascaded down from either side. The skull featured huge, hollow eyes that at night were lit by an eerie green light. A huge crack squiggled down the top of the forehead.

The location soon became a popular photo location from the Skyway buckets that flew overhead. It also served as an outstanding backdrop for publicity photos including one of Mouseketeer Annette attired as Peter Pan standing on the rocks.

Skull Rock and the Pirate Ship became the unintentional victims of the New Fantasyland project in 1982. During the renovation, several rides like Dumbo and King Arthur's Carrousel were relocated. The intention was to do the same with the ship and Skull Rock and move them to the queue area for the Storybook Land Canal Boats.

However, damage to the ship prevented that from happening and removal of Skull Rock was already in progress and too late to stop. Some of the lower rockwork still remains.

In Disneyland Paris, Imagineers Tony Baxter and Chris Tietz recreated Captain Hook's pirate ship as well as a more elaborate Skull Rock in Adventureland. The Disneyland Hotel featured its own smaller version of Captain Hook's ship and Skull Rock done by Tony Baxter and John Stone in its Neverland Pool area starting in 1999 but they were removed by 2011.

Motor Boat Cruise
JUNE 1957—JANUARY 1993

When Disneyland opened, it had a Tomorrowland Lagoon where the Tomorrowland Boats (later renamed the Phantom Boats) operated. The poorly designed fiberglass bodies resulted in the outboard motors overheating and stalling and eventually required a cast member as the captain. There were officially retired in the summer of 1956.

Plans to replace the crafts with airboats proved to be ill-advised after one was tested. However, Walt saw that guests liked the idea of a boat ride and eventually came up with a fleet of motorboats from Arrow Development with the steering wheel in the center so everyone on the large bench seat could have access to it.

The wheel was basically non-functioning but in the early years could be moved just enough that sometimes resulted in the boat getting stuck because it had slid off its rail. The attraction was located between Tomorrowland and Fantasyland, just in front and to the right of where Small World plaza is today and a new canal path was created for the attraction.

The boats were made out of mahogany plywood and painted white with one additional solid color of red, blue, green or yellow on the hull. Exhaust exited under the hull, bubbling up behind the craft so there was no need for a muffler. The motors were Harley Davidson V Twins.

The attraction was on a pipe rail track, so there was no danger steering into the rocks or bridge pylons along the way. A gas pedal did not increase the speed but did produce a louder sound.

There was landscaping and a chance to glimpse some other operating attractions but no storyline and nothing unique to see. When the monorail and the Junior Autopia were opened, the boats cruised under the pylons and bridges for those attractions.

Basically, it was meant to be a passive water version of the popular Autopia attraction. However, it was popular for children because "young skippers can pilot their own private yachts on a cruise through narrow straits and white water rapids with rock-filled currents".

This attraction required a twenty-five cent "B" ticket and, despite its lack of thrills or innovation, lasted for approximately 35 years.

In 1991, to tie in with the Disney Afternoon Avenue promotion, the Motor Boat Cruise was given an inexpensive and brief make-over into Gummi Glen to tie in with the Disney cartoon series *Adventures of the Gummi Bears*. Plywood cutouts of the characters now decorated the banks supposedly helping to tell the story of the bears making Gummi Berry juice.

After the attraction closed in connection with the opening of Mickey's Toontown that needed its operating budget and labor force, the loading platform and nearby grounds became the Fantasia Gardens as an area for guests to take a break or enjoy a snack at the tables and chairs.

Skyway

JUNE 1956—NOVEMBER 1994

The Skyway was not just a method of transportation from one area of the park to another but also an opportunity like the trains to help guest orient themselves to the layout of the park and provide a unique angle for photographs.

The system was the first of its kind in the United States and contained not only new components but also adapted used equipment from two previous events held in West Germany. The cable and drive mechanisms were purchased from ski-lift builder Von Roll Company of Berne, Switzerland.

It took approximately 1,200 feet of cable to connect Fantasyland and Tomorrowland which was supported by four cross-braced towers stretched across the distance.

Imagineer Dick Stine designed the forty-two spun-metal bucket shaped gondolas. Each gondola sat two guests on fiberglass patio chairs bolted to the floor with a pole going down the middle. A one way trip took just over three minutes. The red, blue, yellow and green gondolas swayed forty to sixty feet above the park.

The drive system was inside the Fantasyland station with 35,000 pounds of ballast at the Tomorrowland Station keeping the cable taut. Walt had heard in 1955 about Von Roll Iron Works testing a skyway system.

He bought one before he even knew where it would go and put Imagineer John Hench to work on it with engineers from Von Roll before the end of the year. Walt called it "a transportation system of the future, for use in parking lots in huge shopping centers."

Walt Disney personally opened the attraction on June 21, 1956 at a ceremony at the 5,132 square foot Fantasyland Swiss Chalet decorated like an Alpine garden with Dr. Walter Schmid, the Swiss Consul General of Los Angeles. They rode the first bucket to inaugurate the attraction. It had cost $300,000.

In 1959, with the building of the Matterhorn the gondolas went back and forth through the "glacial grotto" through two openings in the man-made mountain. The Matterhorn now served as the center support.

In 1965 for Disneyland's Tencennial celebration, Bob Gurr re-designed the gondolas into a square shape using lightweight ABS plastic with a steel frame, eliminated the center post, added important safety features and increased the capacity to up to four guests.

In April 1994, Randle Charles fell approximately twenty feet from one of the gondolas and filed a negligence lawsuit against Disney but it was later proven that he had jumped on purpose.

The attraction closed November 9, 1994 and the support towers were removed within a week and the passageway through the Matterhorn was soon sealed up. A costumed Mickey Mouse and Minnie took the last ride while guests watched from below. The Swiss Chalet was demolished June 2016.

New laws required that the attraction be made handicap accessible and the cost for elevators, ramps, room for wheelchairs and more were prohibitive. There were also increasing concerns about liability with guests rocking the gondolas, spitting and throwing things out of them on guests below and some costly structural repairs.

Videopolis
JUNE 1985—JUNE 1995

It was located in an unused meadow off to the west side of the It's A Small World attraction. Disneyland publicity boasted: "The newest, flashiest, most sophisticated electronic dance spot under the stars at Disneyland."

It was a 5,000 square foot open-air dance floor with seventy television monitors layered in a video "wallpaper" effect that showed music videos and images of the guests dancing from three live camera crews.

Those images were often enhanced with special electronics effects to produce "a real time rock video" projected not just on the monitors but on a huge overhead screen.

It had a stage and also featured state-of-the-art sound and video systems. Overhead a giant grid structure lowered from the ceiling. It was adorned with pulsing searchlights. The park purchased some of the staging elements used at a 1984 Los Angeles Olympics facility. There was a snack bar called "Yumz".

It was the first attraction completed under the new Eisner-Wells regime. It was the fastest construction project ever completed by Imagineering taking only a hundred and five days starting from groundbreaking in December 1984.

The rush was because the Tomorrowland Stage had closed to be converted for a theater for the *Captain EO* 3-D movie. Actually, the designers chose the area because they could direct the loud sound away from the park and toward the backstage area.

"Disneyland's all new teenage video dance club phenomenon of neon, flashing lights, special effects, live bands and hot new videos combine in a musical kaleidoscope of sight and sound," stated the publicity.

It was an attempt to draw more teenagers since nearby Knott's Berry Farm was attracting 2,000 teens a night to its Club K.

Filmed live at Videopolis, the Disney Channel had a show in 1987 called *Videopolis* that broadcast concert performances from an array of popular singers and bands. During the day, stage shows were run in Videopolis but at night it became the dance club.

The site attracted a boisterous young teenaged crowd that concerned Disneyland Security at times. Parents and older Disney guests were critical of the nighttime venue. The dance club concept was abandoned in 1989 after several high-profile gang-related incidents.

Permanent seats were installed on the previous dance floor area and it became a venue for a variety of outdoor stage shows:

- The Magic of Christmas (Christmas Seasons 1985–1988)
- Sing'in' Dance'in' Heigh Ho (1987) (Snow White)
- Circus Fantasy (1988)
- Show Biz Is (1989)
- One Man's Dream (December 16, 1989—April 29, 1990) (Walt Disney)
- Dick Tracy in Diamond Double-Cross (June 15, 1990—December 31, 1990)
- Plane Crazy (March 15, 1991 — September 1991) TaleSpin characters
- Mickey's Nutcracker (Christmas seasons 1991 and 1992)
- Beauty and the Beast Live on Stage (April 12, 1992—April 30, 1995

Eventually it was renamed the Fantasyland Theater as a homage to the earlier theater in Fantasyland in 1995 and continued to offer stage shows.

Disney Afternoon Avenue

MARCH 1991—NOVEMBER 1991

The Disney Afternoon was the title of a created-for-syndication two hour block of animated television produced by Walt Disney Television animation and featured four half-hour series. It aired nationwide and in many other countries and was highly popular.

While various different series filled the block from 1990 to 1997, its first season was composed of *Adventures of the Gummi Bears, Duck Tales, Chip'n'Dale Rescue Rangers* and *TaleSpin.* (*Darkwing Duck* replaced *Gummi Bears* in the second season.)

To help promote the programming and to leverage the already growing excitement that had produced the highest ratings, Disneyland transformed the walkway from the Storybook Land Canal Boats to the front of It's A Small World attraction into the Disney Afternoon Avenue.

Guests entered under an archway with a huge hot air ballon with the characters on top. The walkway was now a miniature, cartoon version of Uncle Scrooge's hometown of Duckburg with two dimensional facades that served as themed photo locations where guests could get their pictures taken or meet with costumed characters. The facades were similar in style to the ones at Mickey's Birthdayland in Florida.

Part of the enthusiasm for the new temporary promotion was that guests could meet their favorite characters from the different television series including a Beagle Boy or Don Karnage or the Gummi Bears, characters not usually seen at the park.

Two of the existing attractions got overlays so that the Fantasyland Autopia became the Chip'n'Dale Rescue Rangers Raceway and the Motor Boat Cruise became the Motor Boat Cruise to Gummi Glen, the home of the Gummi Bears. Both rides now featured two-dimensional cutouts of the various characters along the ride as well as new entrance signage.

The Videopolis Train Station was rechristened with a colorful, character filled sign declaring it the Disney Afternoon Train Depot.

Guests could pick up a free Disney Afternoon Live map that had twenty-eight characters in circles encircling its border. Twelve of those circles were incomplete so guests would then go to a dozen locations such as Scrooge's Vault (a pit filled with yellow balls to suggest gold for kids to dive in) or Duckburg City Hall to collect the appropriate character stamp for each circle.

Baloo the bear's dressing room was at a meet-and-greet location in Stage 1 that was under the bridge that now leads to Toontown (since that land had yet to be created) where the train crossed into Fantasyland. Another reason for this temporary land was to test ideas for Mickey's Toontown including a specific meet-and-greet location for Mickey Mouse.

There was a Videocade Game Center where guests could sample the new NES video games based on *DuckTales* and *Rescue Rangers*.

Videopolis featured a stage show with costumed characters Baloo from *TaleSpin*, Chip'n'Dale from *Rescue Rangers* and Launchpad McQuack from *Duck Tales* called *Plane Crazy*. They tried to stop villains Don Karnage and Fat Cat from stealing the X-22 spy plane that they have shrunk (thus the reason for the *Plane Crazy* title).

Mickey's Toontown

When Mickey's Toontown opened in 1993, it was inspired by both the success of Mickey's Birthdayland/Starland at Walt Disney World in Florida and also the feature film *Who Framed Roger Rabbit* (1988) which established that Hollywood animated cartoon characters all lived in their own city called Toontown. It was the newest and smallest land opened at Disneyland.

Even though it has been around a relatively short time compared to the other lands, it has still been the subject of changes and eliminations including the bouncing part of the inflatable Goofy's Bounce House that closed in 1998 and was re-themed as Goofy's Playhouse and Chip'n'Dale's Acorn Pit with its thousands of plastic acorns that was accessed by a slide for children that was also closed in 1998.

When Toontown opened in 1993, CEO Michael Eisner said, "Toontown is an investment, but it's a continuing investment. Disneyland is the tentpole of the entire Walt Disney Company. It is the first attraction that Walt built, and irrespective of anything else we do in the United States, around the world or in California specifically, we will always keep Disneyland changing and growing, and we will continue to invest in it."

Jolly Trolley

JANUARY 1993—APRIL 2009

Even Toons need public transportation and the Jolly Trolley was meant to be a comical interpretation of the fabled Main Street horse trolleys that would go down the center of town as well as the Red Car featured in the film *Who Framed Roger Rabbit* (1988).

It was bright red, with yellow trim, and on top was a big wind-up key just like the toy trolleys that helped inspire its design that constantly turned when the bouncy trolley was in motion.

When the attraction debuted, a second trolley car without the wind-up key was attached to increase capacity but that second car was removed in 1994. The Jolly Trolley bobbed and swayed on a continually twisting track on a one-way, eight hundred foot loop that took a little over two minutes but gave guests a good panoramic view of what was in the land.

Guests sat on benches on either side facing outward. The sign at the boarding area proclaimed: "It's clean! It's fun! It bounces a lot!" What made the trolley jolly was the sound of the music and the giggles as it dipped.

The trolley moved slowly with the conductor constantly ringing the bell to warn clueless guests walking directly in front of it of its approach. Guests could walk faster than the speed of the trolley. It provided a nice sense of ambiance and movement to the area.

According to Disneyland publicity:

> To get the cartoony look to the trolley, Disney Imagineers arranged its wheel sizes so it did not just glide down the tracks of Toontown, but it jiggles, lurches, and weaves.

Several reasons resulted in the Jolly Trolley from stopping its daily trips. First, the wobbly motion of the vehicle to add to the fun put a strain on its parts and it was in need of constant repairs. Second, guests would not get out of the way and the vehicle was slow to stop.

Third, Disney lawyers were concerned about liability issues since there were no restraints to prevent people from simply jumping off or others from jumping on to the moving trolley. Finally, it was so popular that the attraction couldn't handle the capacity that wanted to ride it despite its short length which allowed many multiple trips.

When the attraction closed, the trolley was parked placed next to its station providing a photo opportunity spot. Actually it had always been a good photo opportunity for guests. Photographer Gary Krueger took the 1993 photo of Mickey and his friends on the Jolly Trolley that was sold as the official postcard.

A similar Jolly Trolley ran at Tokyo Disneyland from 1996 to 2009. It was operated by three cast members: a conductor, a person who zigzagged in front of the trolley to clear the way and a third who walked behind to prevent hitchhikers jumping on the moving vehicle.

Tomorrowland

Tomorrowland experienced two major complete overhauls of the land in 1967 and 1998 with many beloved locations disappearing completely and being replaced. Other things that remained had significant changes.

Part of the problem was that Tomorrowland simply could not keep up with the ever-changing future. As the years went on, it was jokingly referred to as Yesterdayland as new discoveries and accomplishments quickly made everything look outdated.

When the newly updated Flight to the Moon attraction opened in 1967 even with NASA's help, much of it became completely obsolete just two years later in 1969 when Apollo 11 landed on the moon. By 1975, at great expense it had to be changed to Mission to Mars.

The final renovation in 1998 was to reformat the land into the retro-future found in old pulp magazines and movies that tried predicting what was coming. Much of the new format was based on the success of Discoveryland at Disneyland Paris.

Just like on Main Street, U.S.A. the original lessees of businesses and exhibits in Tomorrowland were ousted within the first ten years just before the first overhaul. Even popular attractions like the Flying Saucers and the Art Corner were removed.

The Clock of the World

JULY 1955—SEPTEMBER 1966

The Clock of the World stood seventeen feet tall at the entrance to Tomorrowland. Sponsored by Timex (U.S. Time), it was once just as much the icon for that land as the Moonliner and was featured prominently on merchandise and marketing material.

Its design mimicked the look of an hourglass to reinforce that the out-of-the-ordinary looking structure was indeed a clock. There were also hints of elements similar to the late 17th century French urn clock and the illuminated band dial from a mid-18th century lamp clock. It rested on a concrete foundation surrounded by a floral setting suggesting the points of the compass.

The dominant blue Italian glass tile on the icon's base was flecked with silver tiles to suggest the stars in heaven. Above that foundation was a silver conical map showing the world continents.

Early park guests were indeed fascinated that with a little effort it was fairly easy to tell the exact time for any location on Earth twenty-four hours a day but some locations were particularly emphasized like New York, Moscow, Paris and even Disneyland.

When Tomorrowland opened there was a big planter shaped like an eight-pointed star with flags from all 48 states called the Court of Honor. In 1956 the flags and their poles were moved to the entrance of the land and became the Avenue of the Flags leading up to the Clock arranged in the order of their admittance to the Union.

On each flag pole there was a plaque with the name of the state, the date it was admitted to the union and its motto. Three years later two more flags were added. The American flag was placed directly in front of the Clock.

Both the Avenue of Flags and the Clock of the World disappeared in September 1966 to make way for the renovations of Tomorrowland.

At the top of the clock was a half sphere gold anodized aluminum sun and a silver crescent moon with a stylized man in the moon face. At night, lights from within the sun illuminated the moon. These figures rotated clockwise making one revolution a day while the numerical band underneath made of Italian glass mosaic tile rotated counter clockwise and was lit from behind.

Black numerals on a white background signified daylight hours and white numerals on a black background were for the night.

"Herb Ryman had done some drawings for this clock of the future and I did the moon based on the sun Herb had done for the other side of the clock," stated sculptor Blaine Gibson.

Interestingly, at the end of the Adventure Thru Inner Space attraction that debuted in 1967 was a colorful "The World Clock" map projected from the perspective of high above the North Pole and a revolving disk of numerals that told the time anywhere in the world.

20,000 Leagues Under the Sea Exhibit
AUGUST 1955—AUGUST 1966

One of Disney's most popular live action films was *20,000 Leagues Under the Sea* (1954). This exhibit showcasing set pieces and props from the film was a late addition to Tomorrowland to help fill in space. It was located just around the corner from the Monsanto Hall of Chemistry.

Walt hoped to save money by reusing the beautiful sets from the film and to catch the interest of an audience that had never seen movie sets up close especially from a film just released the previous December. The film had won an Oscar for Best Art Direction—Set Decoration in March.

It was intended as a temporary filler to last six months to a year at most while the park found its footing but remained for eleven years. Originally, the exhibit showcased the original diving suits from the movie but they were made of rubber which soon rotted and in the early 1960s were replaced with fiberglass castings of the suits.

Entering the circular exhibit that was only an "A" ticket, the deep voice of actor Thurl Ravenscroft announced "Welcome aboard the submarine Nautilus. You will see the Academy Award winning motion picture sets actually used in the filming of Walt Disney's *20,000 Leagues Under the Sea*". As guests wandered the corridor, they heard in the background the tune *Whale of a Tale* from the film.

The rooms created were the Power Supply Room, Fitting Chamber, Diving Chamber, Pump Room, Wheelhouse, Chart Room, Professor Aronax's Cabin and the Salon: "Here Captain Nemo entertained his guests at the organ...through the starboard viewing port you will see the giant squid which was actually used in the movie."

The squid's arm had been refitted with a more easily maintained cable system and a Hudson eight-cylinder engine to move it. A tin shed had to be built outside the main building to house the massive prop. In the film, the squid had been hacked to pieces by Nemo's crew so the prop needed to have its skin and innards restored by Bob Mattey who had originally made it.

In a frantic effort to try to get the exhibit ready in time for the opening, Walt himself spent time helping spray fluorescent paint on the squid the night before the media day opening.

In the center of the exhibit, guests could peer through windows to see the last resting place of the Nautilus. Walt had wanted to have guides costumed like the crew of the ship take guests through the exhibit but as costs rose that idea was abandoned.

Oceanic props used in the movie and in this exhibit were rented from Marine Props and Rentals in Culver City, California. Extended rental for Disneyland became so expensive that the items were gradually replaced with replicas made at the Studio. The lenses for the bank of lights in the Power Supply Room were actually the bottoms of glass salad bowls.

When the exhibit closed, the organ found a new home in Disneyland's Haunted Mansion ballroom scene.

The Kaiser Hall of Aluminum Fame

JULY 1955—JULY 1960

Because of the late start in designing Tomorrowland, Walt Disney had to rely on exhibits from corporate participants like Richfield Oil, Dutch Boy Paints, Crane Plumbing and others that had only a tentative connection with the world of the future.

This pavilion was a self-guided walk-through exhibit showcasing the history of aluminum products "past, present and future". This attraction was one of the last to be constructed before the park's grand opening, and was completed just days before the gates opened to the public.

Guests began the tour by learning how Kaiser makes aluminum. The pen for the guest book was made out of aluminum. On display was the Kaiser Aluminum Pig (KAP) which is a reference to pig aluminum (the un-milled rough form of aluminum). KAP was three feet tall, wore aluminum overalls, and carried a wrench.

By pushing buttons or pulling handles guests could make "KAP" flat as a pancake, light as a feather, round as a pole, strong as an ox, twisted like yarn, or colored like a rainbow. KAP was able to get sizzling hot, dazzling bright, electronically shocking to demonstrate aluminum's usefulness.

Most impressive was at the entrance was a polished 40-foot aluminum telescope. The exhibit had a series of hallways filled with various aluminum structures, appliances, and showcases, before arriving in an open hall containing the two highlights of the attraction: the "Time Sphere" and the "Brightest Star in the World of Metals", a glowing multi-pointed star that hung high overhead.

The image of the goddess Venus, the "historic symbol of beauty", was re-created life-size in a futuristic setting to represent the welding of art and industry, and the inherent beauty of aluminum. The statue, draped in aluminum yarns and bathed in colored lights, was near a huge multi-colored aluminum star, beneath which were fanciful settings of possible future uses of Kaiser Aluminum like space suits.

The Time Sphere, a massive aluminum ball, projected images of ancient knights, 1950's firemen, and an imagined futuristic spaceman, all proudly using or wearing aluminum.

As guests exited the attraction, they received a commemorative card. The card read:

> (Fill in Your Name) has been ALUMINATED by "The Brightest Star in the World of Metals" at the Kaiser Aluminum Exhibit at Disneyland and is aware of all the benefits pertaining thereto.

Kaiser had convinced Walt that aluminum was truly going to be the metal of the future and so his Autopia cars should have Kaiser aluminum bumpers.

Production problems delayed the delivery of these bumpers until just before Disneyland's opening preventing the chance to do any testing. It quickly became apparent that the soft aluminum crumpled easily when the cars hit each other. Since kids loved bashing other cars on the attraction, the bumpers were quickly replaced.

Kaiser tried to get out of its contract to operate the pavilion as early as October 1957 because they felt the popular weekly *Disneyland* television show was selling commercial time to "competitive sponsors".

Hobbyland / Flight Circle

SEPTEMBR 1955 - JANUARY 1966

Hobbyland opened in the shadow of the Moonliner, basically directly in front of the entrance of the Art Corner, with an enclosed Flight Circle right next to it so that demonstrations would not only provide some kinetic activity to the area but might also encourage sales at the nearby counters.

Hobbyland was a series of plywood booths underneath fiberglass awnings. The shiny Kaiser Aluminum counter tops were filled with model kits with almost every conceivable type of model from dinosaurs to miniature airplanes that flew. The booths also sold the infamous plastic Keppy Kap, the white hardhat of the future decorated with images of all the park's lands.

Disney had an exclusive deal with Strombecker Models to create models based on Disney rides like the Moonliner and the Frontierland Stagecoach so they were prominently displayed. Walt tried to market a gas model engine that he had developed but it never took off.

Walt contacted the local L.A. Hobby and Model Club, to put on demonstrations of models of their custom made, gas-powered planes, cars and boats (in a small pool only twelve inches deep) in a two hundred foot circumference cement circle surrounded by a seven-foot, eleven-inch tall chain link fence.

There was flight tower with a chair for an announcer. Benches and later chairs for guests surrounded the outside area.

Around the four points of the compass marked in its center, demonstrations were supposed to take place but it was an irregular schedule and motors wouldn't start. Wen Mac, a nationally distributed hobby company took over the operation but proved to be even less reliable.

Walt saw that the Cox engines were the only ones that started reliably. In summer 1958, L.M.Cox Manufacturing Co. took over. The deal was that Disney would supply the area rent free and Cox would provide everything else including maintenance of the area.

The Cox employees wearing blue trousers and white shirts worked ten hours a day, four days a week, doing scheduled twenty minute demonstrations generally every half hour, sometimes watched by an approving Walt himself. There were no shows during the winter season until 1964 when the area began operating year round.

The Circle displayed a mini gold colored thimble with a small plane going around the Cox logo. "Thimble Drome" was the name of its line of cars and Control Line planes so it became the Cox Thimble Drome Flight Circle. The employees operated four prop rods and four Mercedes and a variety of model aircraft (sometimes two or three at a time in a dogfight) including the Comanche, the Lil' Stinker bi-plane, the Curtiss Pusher, Super Cub models for Combat, and Cox P-40 Flying Tigers.

Inside the fence, there were tables on which to repair and tweak the models, painted runways for tether cars and airplanes, a carrier deck, and some chairs including one for a young "guest pilot" invited from the crowd for the show. With the remodel of Tomorrowland for 1967, Hobbyland and the Flight Circle area were torn out and became a walkway.

Monsanto House of the Future

JUNE 1957—DECEMBER 1967

In 1953, Monsanto's Plastic Research Laboratory partnered with the Massachusetts Institute of Technology (MIT) to develop a method of using its plastics in house construction. It decided that only a full-scale display house would best demonstrate these new applications both to builders and the public. As a result, it became a free attraction at Disneyland for guests to walk through and discover the wonders of future living.

The house was located to the left side of the entrance to Tomorrowland and was a white cruciform with four gracefully curved fiberglass wings cantilevered from a 256-square-foot central core. It was like a cross or a "plus" sign and not only provided full daylight for each individual room, but sound reduction, privacy, and the ease in adding extra modules.

Each wing was 8-feet tall, 16-feet wide, and 16-feet long. Overall, the house was 1,280-square feet and had three bedrooms, two baths, a living room, a dining room, a family room, and a kitchen. The house opened June 12, 1957 after a media preview a day earlier.

The floors, walls and ceilings were made of plastic. The Kelvinator Division of American Motors Corporation designed the "Atoms for Living Kitchen" that had appliances that either dropped down from overhead, like the "cold zone" units that took the place of a refrigerator, or popped up from the counter, like the new microwave oven.

Sylvania Electric Products Company provided adjustable panel lighting behind polarized plastic ceiling tiles that could mimic "the glow of natural sunlight". Bell Telephone contributed the push-button speakerphone (that would make its general public appearance years later at the 1964 New York World's Fair) with "pre-set" dialing to call selected numbers, like a doctor or the school. In the bathroom there was a phone with a video screen so you could see who was at the front door, but they couldn't see you.

The bathroom featured a movable sink that, at the push of a button, could adjust higher or lower for the person using it. Devices included an electric razor and an electric toothbrush with an attached cord. The living room had a large, wall-mounted (non-working) television screen and, of course, a built-in stereo sound system.

While today, many of these innovations seem quaint and un-exceptional, it must be remembered that at the time they were considered revolutionary.

More than twenty million people (more than the entire pop-ulation of the state of California at the time) visited by the time the house was finally removed in 1967.

The house proved more durable than expected when the original plan for a one-day demolition in late 1967 turned into a long two-week project. The building had to be hack-sawed piece by piece and parts crushed with wrapped chains into removable pieces when the wrecking ball kept bouncing off the sides of the house.

The area was transformed into a beautiful Alpine Garden and later, in 1996, Triton's Garden as the home for Ariel, and in 2008, became Tinker Bell's home of Pixie Hollow.

Adventure Thru Inner Space

AUGUST 1967—SEPTEMBER 1985

Adventure Thru Inner Space gave guests a chance to be miniaturized "beyond the limits of normal magnification." Guests boarded Disney's first omnimover vehicles called "Atomobiles" and went through the "Mighty Microscope" (12-feet high, 37-feet long) into a microscopic world of a snowflake.

The vehicles continued to seemingly diminish in size while guests heard the audio log of the first explorer (actor Paul Frees) helping them understand what they were seeing around them on the 682-foot loop of track.

Eventually, the guests had shrunk to such a tiny size that they confronted the nucleus of the atom (containing a strobe light inside) and had to quickly return to normal size as the snowflake began to melt and find themselves once again in a "world of comfort and convenience, made possible through miracles from molecules." This phrase inspired the theme song "Miracles from Molecules" for the attraction written by the Sherman Brothers.

Even as early as 1957 and the episode of the Disney weekly television show entitled "Our Friend, the Atom," Walt had considered some type of attraction at Disneyland dealing with exploring the world of atoms.

Working with Dr. Charles Allen Thomas, the chairman of the Monsanto Company (that manipulated molecules), the Imagineers decided that frozen water would be the easiest and most understandable concept for guests when explaining molecules.

The omnimovers not only moved people quickly and efficiently through the attraction, but controlled what the audience would see. The curving sides of the vehicle prevented the guests from looking anywhere else besides where the vehicle was facing, as well as creating an acoustical chamber so that the narration could be heard more clearly.

Thomas said:

> We are hoping the excitement generated in our attraction by the creativity of many Disney artists will bring alive the excitement of Inner Space.

Those Disney artists included Imagineer Claude Coats who primarily designed much of the attraction and was known to concentrate on the environment rather than characters in his storytelling.

To make the free attraction more intimate, the Imagineers placed objects like hanging snowflakes within easy reach of the guests in the Atomobiles, which was a huge mistake.

People grabbed at items and even tried to physically destroy them. So the Imagineers came up with the concept now called "Envelope of Protection" meaning when designing future attractions to put things well out of easy reach of guests in a ride vehicle.

The darkness and intimacy of the attraction encouraged everything from covert smoking of marijuana to amorous antics. When the attraction finally closed, an angry guest wrote a complaint letter that included the interesting statement: "How dare you remove it! My son was conceived on that ride!"

The attraction was replaced by Star Tours. The latest version, Star Tours: The Adventures Continue, features the Mighty Microscope visible when escaping the under-construction Death Star above Geonosis.

Submarine Voyage

JUNE 1959—SEPTEMBER 1998

The Submarine Voyage in Tomorrowland was inspired not by the Disney live action film *20,000 Leagues Under the Sea* (1954) but in part by the famous 1958 voyage of the atomic submarine U.S.S. *Nautilus* that had navigated underneath the North Pole. The attraction included a sample of that experience.

Of course, this being Disneyland, guests also got to encounter mermaids, the sunken remains of the lost city of Atlantis and even a friendly, cross-eyed, green sea serpent so it wasn't completely scientifically accurate. However the narration suggested that some of these fantasy elements might just be hallucinations caused by oxygen deprivation from being underwater too long.

That Disneyland fleet included the same names as the actual U.S. submarine fleet: *Nautilus, Seawolf, Skate, Skipjack, Triton, George Washington, Patrick Henry,* and *Ethan Allen.* A total of thirty-eight guests sat in the cramped quarters of each of the 52-foot long submarines and pressed their faces toward the portholes.

The eight original aluminum vessels chugged along at roughly 1.8 miles per hour along 1,635 linear feet of track for a ride that lasted eight minutes and fifteen seconds.

The vehicles were powered by a diesel engine with two guide trunks front and rear with flanged wheels along a rail track. Despite the realistic burst of air bubbles, the vehicles never submerged any further beneath the water.

Guests saw 126 animated figures and 180 static figures as well as approximately 10,000 artificial plants. Because of the chlorine and sunlight, all of these had to be continually repainted.

Construction of the Disneyland Submarine Voyage began in the fall of 1958. The eight submarine hulls were built by the Todd Shipyards of San Pedro. The submarines were then completed at the "Disneyland Naval Yard" in Anaheim under the supervision of Admiral Joe Fowler who had built naval ships during World War II.

The vehicles were painted a military gray giving them an added cache of authenticity. Each one cost approximately $80,625. There was nine million gallons of heavily chlorinated water in the Coral Lagoon that housed the attraction.

The artificial fish performed simple repetitive movements and some were connected to overhead rotating turntables. The guests saw sea turtles, moray eels, lobsters, crabs, sharks, giant clams, an octopus and more.

Amazingly, all these scenes that the guests saw through the portholes were built twice as a mirror image so that a complete set of the same actions were on display for the guests on both the port and starboard side of the ship at the same time.

In 1986, the subs were repainted yellow to indicate they were no longer military vehicles but oceanographic research vessels and were renamed as well. While the attraction closed in 1998 due to continuing maintenance issues and low capacity, it remained in place with constant rumors of it being refurbished and reopened.

In June 2007, it was reformatted as the Finding Nemo Submarine Voyage with elements from the Pixar film *Finding Nemo* (2003) replacing the original show.

Submarine Voyage Live Mermaids

SUMMER 1959, 1965, 1966, 1967

When I interviewed Disney horticulturist Bill Evans in 1985 who had landscaped the Submarine Voyage show building to disguise it, he smiled as he told me:

> One of the things I really miss are the mermaids they used to have at the Submarine Voyage. Those pretty young ladies were very proficient.
>
> They were equipped with a Naugahyde tail section and they had to learn to swim in dolphin fashion. But they couldn't get out of the lagoon. There were always lots of male volunteers including me sometimes to help them and get them out of their tails.

The first mermaids appeared in the lagoon beginning June 1959 to promote the dedication of the attraction. The idea was the brainchild of Disneyland's Entertainment Director Tommy Walker who held auditions for the role at the Disneyland Hotel pool where over a hundred young ladies tried out but only eight were selected.

The inspiration for the mermaids was probably the popular Weeki Wachee Springs live mermaid show where pretty young girls attired as mermaids cavorted underwater while guests viewed them through a huge glass wall. It had been a famous Florida roadside attraction since 1947.

For the official dedication ceremony, eight live mermaids performed a synchronized water ballet seen on an ABC television special, *Kodak Presents Disneyland '59*, shown the following night and in the theatrical featurette *Gala Day at Disneyland* (1960).

Earlier that day, four of the mermaids had appeared on a special float in the Main Street parade where they tossed strands of pearls from King Neptune's treasure chests to guests gathered on the curbs as King Neptune himself sat in a giant shell throne at the front of the float.

When in the lagoon, the mermaids frolicked underwater to the delight of eager guests peering from the submarine portholes. The mermaids could not see inside the vessels but heard the music clearly so could time their appearances accordingly. As part of their training they took turns riding the attraction to see what the guests saw of the mermaids. There was a rock outcropping in the middle of the lagoon where they could bask and wave at guests in between trips underwater.

They could not swim to the guests at the railings because of the underwater track and the path of the submarines. It was also difficult for them to hear over the diesel motors the words of the guests.

The water was not heated but was highly chlorinated that resulted in some of the blonde-haired maids of the sea having their hair turn green.

On Art Linkletter's popular daytime television show, he often asked children what their favorite ride was at Disneyland. One day, a young boy said that his father kept dragging him over to the Submarine Voyage because he liked looking at the live mermaids.

The living mermaids were brought back in the summer of 1965 for Disneyland's 10th Anniversary Tencennial celebration and were so popular that they became a summer attraction through the end of summer 1967.

Mermaid 1959: Susan Musfelt Hoose

In 2012, I interviewed Susan Musfelt Hoose who at the age of seventeen was one of the original 1959 mermaids at Disneyland:

> Requirements were something like: ages 17 to 25, between 5-foot-4 and 5-foot-7, long hair, and be able to swim well. I went to Disneyland Hotel pool where tryouts were being held. Each girl wearing a swimsuit was individually told to stand at the deep end of the pool while her arms were tied with a soft cloth above her head in a diving position; her legs were tied at the knees, then the ankles. We were instructed to use the dolphin movement (up and down body movement with a huge kick) once we hit the water to propel ourselves underwater to the shallow end. Four lifeguards were positioned on either side of the pool.

> Eight of us were picked. All of our four hour practices were at the hotel pool, because the lagoon at the park was still under construction. We were paid about $45 a week in two-week increments. Minimum wage in 1959 was $1.00 an hour, so we thought we were millionaires.

> We practiced diligently for weeks. The three pound tail and halter top were especially made to fit each girl and were color coordinated. I wore Kelly green.

> To put on the tail, we sat on the ground and put our feet into the tail, which were actually rubber flippers. Then we would flip over on our stomach, while one of the other girls would zip us up. The invisible zippers ran from our heels to our waist. At this point, we simply rolled over, off the edge, and into the water. Once in the water we could maneuver with relative ease.

> In the near-freezing 50-degree water you could never warm up, even on a sunny California summer afternoon. I think we worked Thursday through Sunday because that's when there was the most attendance.

> We also had to contend with the danger of getting too close to the huge submarine propellers. When our hour was up, we would

dive underwater, swim out of sight of the public into the show building and be lifted out of the water by two men stationed on the dock. The next girls would be dropped into the water and replaced us in a smooth transition, hour after hour, until the end of our shift which was before dark.

The largest rock in the lagoon where we rested in the sun and tried to thaw out from the cold water was quite some distance from the crowd. We never experienced any inappropriate behavior or things being thrown at us and we couldn't hear what they were yelling at us.

Some of the girls got terribly sunburned and the chlorine turned the blondes' hair green. The chlorine bothered everyone but it was considered part of the job. The high chlorine content was necessary to keep the water pristine—and we accepted that.

Mermaid 1966: Edie

In 2011, I interviewed Edie who worked as a Disneyland mermaid in 1966 and 1967:

> My high school friend, Robin, had been a mermaid in 1965 but couldn't do it in 1966. She said that I would be perfect for the job so I went to the tryout at the Disneyland Hotel pool. Five of us were selected plus one girl from the year before, Jini, who was our supervisor.

> Basically we were told they were looking for girls who could swim, smile, had long hair and out-going personalities. We did two lengths of the freestyle, and lengths of one or two other strokes wearing the tails from the previous year.

> It was Judy, Lynn, Marcia, Cynthia, Jini and myself. We worked in shifts of two at a time for an hour in the water and an hour out. Jini taught us how to swim dolphin-style, and how to keep bubbles from coming out of our mouths, plus basics about what to do while sitting on the rock, and underwater when the Subs went by.

> The Productions Department measured us from hip to toe for neoprene tails, complete with large flukes, and green starfish bras. We were each individually fitted for our tails. There was only one for each girl, no back ups. We were taught to slither into the Submarine Lagoon from a hidden chamber and dolphin kick underwater to magically surface in the center of the pool. There we sat on a rock and untangled our hair with immense blue and yellow plastic combs, and plucked ersatz wooden lyres that made no sound.

> Each time a submarine passed, we dove underwater to frolic about, hang upside down by spinning our tails, and to wave at curious faces plastered against the portholes. For all this we were paid $1.85 an hour—a whopping net of $59.55 each week.

> The first shift would be in the water by the time the park opened and we worked for a total of eight hours a day. We got into our costumes in a tunnel inside the park at the lagoon, where we kept our tails during the day. We performed five days a week.

We *did* experience dry skin, discoloring and dryness of our hair, and skin, sunburn and some problems with opening our eyes underwater because of the chlorine. Some of the blondes had trouble with their hair turning green.

Each weekend sailors draped over the handrails around the Lagoon, ogling with off-duty exuberance. They rolled quarters inside dollar bills and tossed them into the lagoon for us to retrieve. One young hero flung himself into the water and swam to our rock. He basked between us, waving to his howling buddies, until Security retrieved him. I never had anyone throw anything but money, and it was almost always the sailors just trying to get a smile—so that was fine. I never once thought of it as a circus animal act. No one tossed food or popcorn. We kept the money.

Submarine Voyage Other Mermaids

JULY 1959—SEPTEMBER 1988

In the Submarine Voyage attraction three similar mermaids swam around in a circle while three others examined the many treasures spilled from sunken ships on the bottom of the ocean floor. Imagineer Marc Davis designed all six and Bob Sewell installed them so they moved correctly.

Scupltor Blaine Gibson told Leon and Jack Janzen:

> In 1959, I sculpted the mermaids for the Submarine Voyage. Those first underwater figures beame more like amoebas than mermaids because of the oxidation of the coloring and the material that we had. Then Jack Ferges and I did the next set of mermaids.

Ferges and Gibson, both former Disney animators, sculpted them for a couple of weeks in B-Wing of the Animation Building at the Disney studio. Walt decided not to have the mermaids wear seashell bras and not to put nipples on their rounded breasts.

The moving crew arrived to move the figure to the backlot so a cast could be made. However, as it was being wheeled down Dopey Drive, the figure toppled over and crashed to the ground, damaging it beyond possible repair.

When word got back to them, rather than being angry, Ferges and Gibson broke out into laughter. Gibson said it was great because now they could do a better version because neither man liked the original but felt deadline pressure to get it done quickly.

Harriet Burns explained to Leon and Jack Janzen:

> Blaine sculpted them out of clay. We eventually cast them in duraflex. I was trying to come up with a 'skin' for the meramids that would hold applied color. I put thickener in it and flexible-izer and tried many different pigments.
>
> We attempted to paint the skin but once it was underwater, it would peel off! I had to actually "fuse" it onto the pigment of the mermaid with a torch. If I got the torch too close to her skin, it

would make a big pockmark, but if you didn't get it close enough, it wouldn't fuse.

So, it was a layer on top of the druaflex, fused to the mermaid. They took a lot of time and they were heavy. They weighed from sixty to eighty pounds each. I'd have to haul them across the floor, and put them up on the plaster mold that was standing up and then rope them onto that mold.

Then I torched the thing. All the green scales—all of that. It was not a quick process and I had to make and attach the wigs seperatedly. I made a cap and attached nylon hair onto that. As a test, I put the purple, green and pink wigs in straight Clorox for two weeks and they didn't fade.

Then when we got it out in the Submarine Voyage, it faded immediately because of all the chemicals and chlorine in the water. So then I had them extrude the nylon with the pigment in it. That eventually worked.

Viewliner

JUNE 1957—SEPTEMBER 1958

Walt desperately wanted to showcase some new form of transportation in Tomorrowland. General Motors was promoting a new type of streamlined, lightweight train dubbed the Aerotrain that was described as "a prototype interurban express train of the future." It was hoped it would encourage travelers to return to train travel. Two such trains started operation in 1956.

Just as it sponsored the Santa Fe & Disneyland Railroad and would later sponsor the Alweg Monorail, Santa Fe agreed to sponsor a half-scaled version of the actual Aerotrain done for Disneyland by Imagineer Bob Gurr.

The Viewliner consisted of an "engine," four coaches, and an observation coach at the rear. The Viewliners were designed, engineered, and assembled at the Disney Studios in Burbank.

Each of the coaches measured 16 feet 10 inches in length, with a capacity of 32 passengers, and weighed 1,980 pounds. The bodies were constructed out of aluminum on steel frames and had conventional railroad wheels that operated on a 30-inch gauge track. The Disneyland steam locomotives ran on a 36-inch gauge track.

There were two Viewliners: a red one that operated out of Tomorrowland and a blue one that operated out of Fantasyland. Both Viewliners maneuvered around a track loop that at one point paralleled the track of the steam trains.

The names of the Fantasyland cars were Alice, Cinderella, Pinocchio, Bambi, and Tinker Bell. The names of the Tomorrowland cars were Jupiter, Venus, Mars, Mercury, and Saturn.

The engine was unique because it was a 1954 Oldsmobile 88 coupe. There was a 14-inch section in the center of the dashboard for a radio that had to be removed so that the chassis was not too wide for the track. That's why examining photos of the front of the train show a seam down the middle of the windshield.

It had a steering wheel (that Gurr moved over to the other side), automatic transmission, reverse gear, and brakes. It operated on gasoline and ran on a standard Oldsmobile Rocket V8 engine. The engine was 18 feet 10 inches in length and weighed approximately 5,000 pounds.

Walt had the two speedometers calibrated to the scale of the train so when it reached its top speed of 30 mph, the speedometers showed 120 mph.

The actual trains in use in major cities turned out not to gain favor with anyone (especially since the savings of using them were not passed on to the passengers) and eventually ceased operations.

The Disneyland attraction lasted only 15 months until September 30, 1958. During its short career, the vehicles carried 1,452,870 guests and required a "B" ticket.

Walt attempted to donate the vehicles to be used as parking lot trams for the new Dodger stadium and, when that offer was turned down, he suggested that they be used as a shuttle between the stadium and Griffith Park. That suggestion was also rejected.

The two Viewliners were actually kept in a storage shed behind Fantasyland until the late 1970s when they were eventually scrapped.

WEDWay PeopleMover

JULY 1967—AUGUST 1995

The WEDWay PeopleMover was a continuously moving, intermediate-speed transportation system not dependent on an internal combustion engine but on silent electric motors in the track itself presented by Goodyear that Walt intended to use in his EPCOT project.

When Disneyland opened in 1955, the steam trains went nonstop around the entire perimeter of the park on a "Grand Circle Tour" to allow guests a glimpse at what was actually there.

The PeopleMover system was to provide the same function of showing guests an inside glimpse of the 1967 New Tomorrowland attractions in a leisurely sixteen minute ride in 62 four-car trains that were colored blue, red, green and yellow and ran non-stop on an elevated track.

The term PeopleMover was simply a casual placeholder identification suggested by Walt himself, because the vehicle moved people. He assumed that his staff would eventually come up with a better name, but that never happened. Like the monorail, Walt hoped that the system would be adopted for urban transit in cities.

The attraction was an updated version of a system developed by Imagineering for the Ford Magic Skyway attraction at the 1964-65 New York World's Fair. Ford did not want to sponsor the ride at Disneyland, since it promoted a form of transportation that could replace Ford automobiles. Goodyear, maker of tires including the ones used on the attraction, became its sponsor instead.

Roughly every nine feet, the vehicle passed over one of 517 electric motors in the three-quarter mile long track that would turn a tire. The tires turn against the bottom of the vehicle, propelling the vehicle forward up to a speed of six miles per hour. Guests boarded on a rotating platform moving at the same speed so the vehicles seemed almost motionless.

It was Walt's intention that the PeopleMover would eventually carry citizens of EPCOT from their homes to shopping areas, to their work in the centralized hub of the city and more, without having to use cars. Doing so would eliminate air and noise pollution, traffic jams, save energy and much more.

On either side of the train were two facing 54-foot-long tile murals on buildings depicting children done by artist Mary Blair, familiar for her similar work on the It's A Small World attraction.

One mural was on the CircleVision 360 building representing global communication. The other was on the Adventure Thru Inner Space building representing different types of energy (sun, sea, sky, and water). Collectively, they were known as "The Spirit of Creative Energies Among Children."

Imagineer John Hench was the major influence in the re-design of the exterior of the New Tomorrowland and, on the PeopleMover, he was attempting to create a more organic approach that would welcome guests to the future. He worked closely with sculptor Mitsu to have soft symmetrical arches.

This approach can clearly be seen on the PeopleMover, where he had the support columns resemble curving tree branches with softened shapes and edges. The attraction was replaced by the short-lived Rocket Rods.

Moonliner

JULY 1955—SEPTEMBER 1966

The project leader for the iconic Tomorrowland Moonliner was Imagineer John Hench who consulted with scientists Willy Ley and Wernher von Braun.

Their input influenced the design of the spaceship with its white fuselage and red highlights to look similar to the infamous V2 rocket that von Braun had developed during World War II in Nazi Germany. However, Hench included his own design elements like the three twenty-two foot long steel pylons flaring out at the base of the cylinder for support.

The rocket was 72 feet tall (80 feet with the legs) and was estimated to be one-third what the actual size of the rocket might be to hold 102 passengers. The exterior featured 15,000 square feet of aluminum.

In an edition of the *Los Angeles Times,* it announced:

> Wednesday, July 6, 1955. Early risers along a twenty-mile route between Hollydale and Anaheim were startled this morning to see an 80 foot Rocket ship moving through the streets. In order to prevent a gigantic traffic tie-up, the ten ton aluminum and steel "Air Ship of Tomorrow" was trucked before sun-up, from Hollydale where it was built, to Disneyland where it will become part of the TWA exhibit as well as the theme of the Tomorrowland section of the park.

The Moonliner was sponsored by Trans World Airlines (TWA). According to Disneyland publicity in 1955: "Towering high above all else in Tomorrowland, the TWA Moon Rocket symbolizes Trans World Airlines' interest in future air travel and planned scientific progress."

Walt Preston was a civil engineer who developed the structural engineering drawings necessary for the assembly of the rocket pylon. Waldrip Engineering was put in charge of acquiring materials and doing the actual construction and contracted with Preston to do the detailed shop drawings and with his assistant Jim Block overcoming the challenges of the expansion and contraction of the exterior in the heat and cold as well as the overturning forces of wind and earthquake.

"The rocket symbolizes the scientific achievements that will be as familiar to the young people of tomorrow as Main Street is to you and me," Walt told reporter Florabel Muir for an article in the July 10, 1955 edition of the *Daily News*.

The sponsorship shifted in 1962 to McDonnell Douglas when TWA owner Howard Hughes sold his interest in TWA and that company decided to end its sponsorship. McDonnell Douglas painted its name on the rocket and replaced the horizontal red stripes with vertical blue ones, destroying the forced perspective Hench had originally created that made the rocket look taller.

With the renovation of Tomorrowland, a two-thirds size replica (roughly fifty-three feet high on a twelve foot pedestal) was placed on the roof of the Spirit of Refreshment building, sponsored by Coca-Cola whose colors are red and white, next to Redd Rockett's Pizza Port. It is approximately fifty feet from the original location of the icon.

Flying Saucers
AUGUST 1961—SEPTEMBER 1966

The Flying Saucer attraction did provide great fun for the over five million guests fortunate enough to ride this modern version of carnival bumper cars.

A guest would board one of the 64 one-person saucer vehicles designed by Bob Gurr and would be lifted by pressurized air from valves on the 16,000 square foot metal arena floor and could hover. Gurr described it to me as "a human air hockey rink". Each saucer had a lap belt like the ones on the Autopia.

By leaning, the guest could control the direction but not the speed of the vehicle. As the pilot leaned, the saucer would tip slightly in that direction, decreasing the gap between it and the floor and allowing air to escape in the opposite direction thus propelling the craft.

The blue-floored arena had two sides that operated somewhat independently. A large boom would sweep across half the circle, collecting saucers and maneuvering them back to the loading area while the just-loaded saucers started their ride. It operated continuously so a group was always loading or unloading while another was gliding and bumping into each other on the floor.

Hovercraft vehicles were very popular at the time and a German inventor brought one of his versions to the Disney Studios to try and sell it to Walt Disney. Gurr who had become responsible for all moving Disneyland vehicles took it for test run on the backlot. While it handled well, Gurr worried the high speed razor-sharp blades were not safe in the general public and the individual motor might fail under the demands of constant use.

Gurr created a design that was basically an overturned bowl with no moving parts. He added two handles by the seat for guests to grip but they had no effect on the movement. Arrow Development who had built many Disneyland attractions including the Matterhorn Bobsleds developed the arena. Four 100 HP motors supplied 300,000 cubic feet of air per minute pressure underneath the arena that was covered with thousands of damper baffles that would open and close to control the air flow to different sections of the floor.

As a saucer approached a given area, the air pressure under the saucer would increase, lifting the saucer by inches.

There were difficulties with the attraction from the start and in fact, it did not even open on schedule. The dynamics of this scale pneumatic system were pretty much unknown so the constant bouncing sometimes introduced a vibration like an echo upsetting the flow of air and caused the system to stop. The sudden drop in air pressure would create a sound like a sonic boom heard throughout the park. Guests who were too heavy had difficulty lifting the vehicle and guests who were too light could not properly move it.

Lack of dependability, limited capacity and the plans for the remodeling of the new Tomorrowland to open in 1967 with new attractions resulted in the attraction being closed. Space Mountain later occupied the same space.

Rocket to the Moon

JULY 1955—SEPTEMBER 1966

Sponsored by Trans World Airlines (TWA), the Rocket to the Moon attraction was delayed from operating on opening day by four days due to severed electric cords by a disgruntled electrical worker that had to be rewired.

There was great curiosity and interest in the possibility of manned space flight so Walt Disney knew that guests would be interested in a "science factual" exploration of the topic.

Scientist Willy Ley was working with director Ward Kimball on the Tomorrowland episodes for the Disney television show about outer space and was loaned to the attraction to help out with some of the concepts (like the ship flipping over in space) and his input helped shaped what the guests saw and gave it an aura of credibility.

John Hench was responsible for painting the backgrounds that were seen as the spaceship took off from the Earth with some assistance from matte painter Peter Ellenshaw. Hench was also responsible for the design of the Moonliner which was similar to the spaceship that guests were supposedly boarding.

Guests entered a double hemisphere building where they would soon board the Star of Polaris spaceship piloted by Captain Collins. They waited in a briefing room for fifteen minutes watching a film of a brief history of space exploration and a preview through the use of animation and models of their trip around the moon.

Then roughly 104 guests followed a corridor meant to be the gantry tunnel they had just seen in pre-show into a three-tiered circular seating theater that was meant to be the passenger compartment of the spacecraft. At the center of both the ceiling and the floor of the theater were large, round "scanner screens" where film was back projected of the flight. In this way, guests could view where they had come from and where they were going as if they were portholes.

Realistic sound effects throughout the journey around the moon added to the illusion as did Captain Collins reassuring and informative narration. At appropriate times the seats vibrated and air jacks under the seats helped with the sense of losing gravity.

Highpoints of the flight included a view of the dark side of the moon temporarily illuminated by flares from the ship (and it looks exactly like the side of the moon that had always been seen) and the minor emergency returning to the Earth when a shower of meteoroids hit and caused some minor damage to the ship.

Much of the material and models like the image of the rotating space station were borrowed from Kimball's television show *Man and the Moon* that first aired in December 1955 and was finishing production. It featured a trip around the moon very similar to the attraction including lighting up the dark side with flares.

Douglas Aircraft took over the sponsorship of the attraction from 1962–1966 and continued with the revamped and updated Flight to the Moon attraction that opened in 1967.

Flight to the Moon
AUGUST 1967—JANUARY 1975

The New Tomorrowland that opened in 1967 featured several new attractions and the popular Rocket to the Moon ride was significantly updated into Flight to the Moon sponsored by McDonnell Douglas. Aerospace manufacturer Douglas Aircraft Company merged with the McDonnell Aircraft in 1967 to form McDonnell Douglas.

The Moonliner and the building for Rocket to the Moon were demolished in 1966. The new Flight to the Moon building took over the space that had previously been the Flying Saucers attraction and is now the location of Redd Rockett's Pizza Port.

Inside were two similar but larger "Lunar Transports" theaters meant to represent the passenger cabins that were larger in diameter (for 162 guests) with slightly wider seats and with a fourth concentric circle of seats in each of them.

The four and a half minute pre-show was now a terraced walkway with railings on each level. To the right were huge glass panels that allowed guests to see pre-launch activity in Mission Control, "the nerve center of Disneyland's spaceport". Eight audio-animatronics male figures were seated along two banks of computers moving their heads and arms.

The one standing figure who talked to the audience was Control Center Director Mr. Tom Morrow with his lower torso conveniently hidden by a computer. It was the first time that an audio-animatronics figure interacted with a live host even though it was tightly scripted.

Screens behind Mr. Morrow showed some NASA footage, new projects that were being prepared and the preparations for Flight 92 (that the guests would soon be boarding for their flight) as well as the famous footage from runway 12 where a clumsy albatross came in for an awkward landing that tripped security alarms.

Once in the theater, the upper ceiling and lower floor projection screens showed some of the same material from the original attraction with flares lighting up the dark side of the moon and being caught in a meteoroid shower on the return to the Earth. However, during the nine minute moon flight, two screens mounted on opposite sides of the cabin's walls showed a new "live" telecast from the moon's surface of astronauts gathering ore samples, demonstrating weightlessness and showing off the nearby moon base.

Just two years later, on July 20, 1969, the attraction became instantly obsolete with the Apollo 11 mission having American astronauts walking on the surface of the moon.

While Disneyland publicity proclaimed, "Disney called on NASA experts from the McDonnell Douglas Corporation to provide data. The new show is as scientifically authentic, accurate and up-to-date as possible", NASA had purposely withheld information including the actual design of the moon landing vehicle.

From July 1969 through December 1972, six manned missions of NASA's Apollo program landed on the Moon resulting in dwindling attendance for the attraction that closed and was reformatted as Mission to Mars. Walt Disney World had a similar Flight to the Moon attraction in Magic Kingdom's Tomorrowland from 1971–1975 but it was not sponsored by McDonnell Douglas.

Mission to Mars

MARCH 1975—NOVEMBER 1992

While the Mission to Mars attraction at first glance seemed to be a simple overlay to the just closed Flight to the Moon attraction, there were some differences beyond changing the destination to a fly-by of the red planet Mars.

The entrance and holding areas were redone with new colors, signs and photographs. The flight number had changed from #92 to #295. More importantly, a female audio-animatronics character took over one of the seats in the Mission Control pre-show that had previously been all male.

Mr. Tom Morrow must have gotten promoted or retired because he was replaced by the audio-animatronics bespectacled Mr. Johnson (who was voiced by actor George Walsh who had previously supplied the voice for Mr. Morrow) with his headset and clipboard discussing space travel and the Mars vehicle. The new show included Mars footage shot by a NASA satellite.

Of course, there was no base on Mars for astronauts to transmit a "live" broadcast to the guests. So that section was changed to images from probes launched from the rocket and narrated by Third Officer Collins voiced by Peter Renoudet. Those probes showed details of the surface of the planet including canyons and mountains.

Some things that had delighted guests in the previous show remained including the footage of the albatross tripping the security alarms and the danger from a meteoroid shower forcing the ship's immediate return to earth.

The theaters remained the same as an earlier incarnation with four tiers and screens on the top and bottom. However, when the moon came into view, the ship jumped into "hyper-space penetration" that brought Mars into range.

Some guests had lost interest in real space flights so weren't as interested in this new adventure and attendance quickly dwindled.

It was planned that the attraction would be replaced as part of the Disneyland Tomorrowland 2055 project with the new ExtraTERRORestrial Alien Encounter attraction as was done with Walt Disney World's Mission to Mars attraction. It was cancelled due to massive cost overruns of EuroDisneyland (now Disneyland Paris).

The building was vacant for awhile and eventually became the home to the Toy Story Funhouse (January 1996 to May 1996) where guests could wander through several rooms to play video games, experience an obstacle course wearing pads like the Green Army Men, interact with different displays and have photos taken with the costumed Toy Story characters Woody and Buzz Lightyear and more.

The Toy Story Funhouse was not created specifically for Disneyland but had been part of "Totally Toy Story" at the El Capitan Theater in Hollywood to help promote the original release of the film.

Chairman of the Walt Disney Studios Dick Cook began an initiative to turn theme park attractions into films and one of the projects he approved was Brian De Palma's *Mission to Mars* (2000) The finished film has little direct relationship to the attraction but did inspire the Mission: SPACE attraction at Epcot in Florida with actor Gary Sinise playing the same role he did in the film.

Rocket Jets

JULY 1967—JANUARY 1997

The Astro-Jets that opened in March 1956 was actually a popular amusement park spinner ride called The Super Roto-Jet built by the Klaus Company in Memmigen, Bavaria. The rotating base was actually a converted World War II German artillery gun that could rotate 360 degrees and raise and lower the stubby little cylinders with tiny wings and an open cockpit.

Disney paid $200,000 for it. For the dedication ceremony, Disneyland invited jet pilots from El Toro Marine Air Station, the 11th Naval District Headquarters in San Diego and the Army Air Force Base at Long Beach to be the first pilots. Each pilot was accompanied by a child who was visiting Disneyland that day.

Each jet was on an arm extending out about twenty feet from the central column and guests could coax the height with a lever in the cockpit up to thirty-eight feet. The attraction was on the ground like the similar Dumbo attraction but it spun faster and higher.

The fleet of twelve ships each had a name selected by John Hench: Canopus, Vega, Sirius, Castor, Regulus, Pica, Capella, Arcturus, Rigel, Spica, Proycon, Altair and Antares. They were painted white with red or blue trim.

The name and nothing else was changed to the Tomorrowland Jets on August 1964 because American Airlines was using the term "Astro Jets" for their new fleet of passenger planes. United Airlines complained because they were spending quite a bit of money sponsoring the Enchanted Tiki Room while one of their competitors was receiving free publicity. Dick Irvine agreed and authorized the name change.

The attraction closed in 1966 in preparation for the New Tomorrowland. In 1967 the Rocket Jets debuted. There was an eighty-five foot tall tower designed by George McGinnis to resemble a NASA Saturn V rocket (the real Saturn V rockets began space service in 1967) and surrounding it near the top were twelve, two-passenger Apollo-style rocket jets that flew sixty feet above the ground.

The rockets vehicles were colored orange/red, black, and white and were mounted on eighteen foot long control arms. Guests had to board the attraction by using one of the two gantry elevators to get to the upper level above the PeopleMover station.

This design did not fit in with the retro-future concept for the latest incarnation of Tomorrowland so the attraction space was replaced in 1998 by The Observatron which is a kinetic sculpture with satellite dishes on arms supposedly to communicate with outer space. A new rocket spinner attraction at ground level called the Astro Orbitor debuted in 1998 as well. Originally, it was meant to be on the Rocket Jets platform but it was too heavy and larger so was located to the front of the land. Similar outer space spinner attractions exist in five Disney theme parks worldwide.

Tomorrowland Space Girl
AUGUST 1955—1965

To provide added value to his new park and to suggest that Disneyland was not just a theme park but a series of movie sets, in the earliest years of the park, Walt Disney employed live performers associated with particular areas of the park to provide an interactive experience with guests.

In Frontierland, Sherrif Lucky (named after retired Los Angeles police officer "Lucky" Fauntz who originated the role) helped keep law and order in the Wild West even if it meant four gunfights a day with a crooked goateed gambler named Black Bart in the street.

Robin Hood and some of his Merry Men, inspired by the 1952 Disney live-action movie of the Sherwood Forest archer, sometimes hung around the entrance of Sleeping Beauty Castle.

In Tomorrowland, there was a Space Man and a Space Girl who wandered throughout the area and greeted guests. Over the years, several different performers played those roles and the costumes changed, as well. One of the men in the Space Man costume was Randy Bright who later became an Imagineer. On Opening Day, Don MacDonald was the performer in the costume and in 1961, Gordon McClymont wore the suit.

The Space Man was designated "K-7" on his helmet and the Space Girl was known as "K-8" suggesting that they might have an unseen pet dog who was designated "K-9". They were considered the "symbols of Tomorrowland" and with a paucity of attractions in the landin the earliest days, they were encouraged to talk with guests, take souvenir photos with them and sometimes ride the attractions to try to enhance the idea of the future.

Since this was before the time of manned space flight, the word "astronaut" did not yet exist which is why the designation "Space" was used since that was common in books and movies of the time. "Girl" was a common term at the time for an attractive young woman. In 1961, Donna Fox who previously worked at the Coke Corner was the Space Girl.

The space outfits were hardly authentic nor represented the science-factual world of the future just around the corner that Walt was trying to promote. The costumes were the type of exaggerated fashion seen in popular sci-fi television and movies of the 1950s.

The clothing was white with metallic highlights and the over-sized transparent glass helmets that resembled overturned fish bowls featured antenna on top. There were little Astro Jet packs strapped to their backs and both wore silver boots. Space Girl's boots had high heels. At one point, Space Girl wore a mini-skirt which would not protect her from the coldness of space and a cape but was very much in keeping with the style seen by women portraying roles in outer space in comic books, pulp magazines, television, and movies.

One requirement was that the performers were to be at least six feet tall or taller to make them stand out even more and to suggest that in the future people had subtle differences from contemporary people.

Space Girl 1964: Terry Jo Steinberger

In 2014, I interviewed Terry Jo Steinberger who portrayed the Space Girl in 1964:

> After graduation, I applied for a job at Disneyland in September 1964. I was asked if I wanted to be the Space Girl. The interviewer just said, "You walk around Tomorrowland in a costume, cordially greeting quests and take pictures with them." That was the only description Disney ever gave me about the character and what was expected.

> The implication was that we were tall people from the future. I guess people in the future were going to be taller for some reason. We weren't given any particular names, just Space Man and Space Girl.

> Fortunately, I fit the costume, which was a dress, cape and high-heeled silver boots which were a little loose. It was lucky I fit the costume because they only had one of them, no backups.

> There were no backup performers for our characters, but we never got sick and were always there. The dress was lined inside with cotton but some kind of silver metallic fabric on the outside. It was really quite comfortable.

> I was bare legged. I wore a helmet and Astro Jets on my back. It wasn't difficult to breathe or talk wearing the helmet. There was a hole in the middle of the front that people could not easily see for us to breathe.

> I was probably making minimum wage, like everyone else, although I don't remember exactly. Nor do I remember what my working shift was like. Maybe six to eight hours each day.

> I think we were allowed two fifteen minute breaks during the day and a lunch. We went backstage for breaks and there were picnic tables there. We took off our helmets. We would sometimes take "secret breaks" high in the rafters of the 20,000 Leagues exhibit.

> Pete had been hired long before I was and he helped me tremendously. He was about 6-foot 9-inches tall and I was only about

5-foot 11 3/4-inches tall. He taught me the most important thing about the job was to have a good sense of humor about it. He and I sometimes stood motionless, posing as statues, and then suddenly moved our eyes and scared the guests.

Our supervisor reprimanded us and said, "Stop doing that! You could give someone a heart attack!" But we still did because it was fun, just not very often.

I think mostly I just said, "Hi!" or "Welcome to Tomorrowland!" I asked if they were having fun and answered their questions about the rides and where they were. I sometimes asked if they had seen Mickey Mouse.

I worked as Space Girl for part of that winter and then I broke my collar bone skiing at Snow Valley Ski Area in San Bernardino Mountains during Christmas 1964, and could not bear the weight of the helmet because it was too much for my collar bone so they moved me over as a parade performer.

Space Girl 1965: Carol Farris

In 2012, I interviewed Carol Farris, the last performer to play Space Girl in Tomorrowland:

> I was just a little over six foot one and a job at Disneyland sounded like fun. The short dress from the previous girl fit and the high heel boots were a fit, as well and I started two days after my interview as Space Girl. They explained that Pete who played the Space Man would fill me in.
>
> I was Space Girl at Disneyland for about a year and a half until late 1966 and, from what I remember, we were the last space couple. Pete was I think 6'9" with at least a two to three inch sole on his shoes, and then the helmet, and my heels were at least two to three inches high—we were pretty daunting in appearance.
>
> Guests would just stand by us and hurriedly take a picture. We didn't get asked for autographs as I remember. Depending on how we felt on any given day, we would choose how much we wanted to interact as far as conversation.
>
> The job was just walking around pretending to be an astronaut, posing for pictures and visiting with guests. Usually, it was an eight-hour shift, working about five-and-a-half hours on stage with several off-stage breaks in between to make sure we wouldn't be overwhelmed from the sun on hot days. We weren't supposed to leave Tomorrowland.
>
> The dress I wore was silver and made of light breathable material, so it was never uncomfortable. We didn't have another back up costume. Our helmets could get uncomfortable on exceptionally hot days, but our breaks were so frequent, it was never a struggle.
>
> Disney laundered it and made sure all was in good condition for the next appearance. We also didn't have a substitute in case of illness, but I don't remember either one of us not being there for our work days, which was usually about four days a week.
>
> On our workday, we were supposed to be in public view at all times, except on breaks. On hot days we would cruise through

the Pac Bell exhibit for some cool air.

One exhibit we weren't allowed to enter was 20,000 Leagues Under the Sea. Our space persona didn't really fit with the theme of the exhibit. However, periodically, we would venture in. Midway in the exhibit, at an entry into a following room, we would appear as statues with our hands extended inviting the guests to shake. The lighting being dark, our costumes appeared almost as underwater suits.

We were so tall that I don't think the guests even looked at our helmets. They were so impressed with how "real" we looked. Guests would shake our hand and freak, calling over friends to explain how terrific Disney was in creating such realness to their exhibit characters. We towered over everyone so they never noticed us trying to hold back our laughter.

The Art Corner

OCTOBER 1955—SEPTEMBER 1966

When Disneyland opened in July 1955, the Art Corner was set up in a striped tent just off of the entrance of hub near the Red Wagon Inn. It was soon relocated into a permanent building near Hobbyland. The exterior had a patchwork of large colorfully designed squares. The interior was decorated like an outdoor Parisian art market. Jack Olsen (who supplied art supplies to the Disney studio) ran the shop.

It was Olsen who rescued cels from the dumpsters at the studio where they had been tossed after being filmed, cut them down to image size, and prepared them for sale at Disneyland with a rectangular gold sticker on the back that read:

> This is an ORIGINAL Celluloid drawing actually used in a Walt Disney Production. Released exclusively at Disneyland.

He sold thousands of them. Some of them were on spinner racks and cost as little as a dollar and half each with a background and a cardboard matte.

According to Disneyland:

> The Art Corner carries a complete line of artists' material for both professionals and beginners, as well as many special items designed by the artists at the Walt Disney Studio for exclusive distribution by the Art Corner.

Merchandise exclusively sold at The Art Corner included six cartoon character guides put together under the supervision of animator Paul Carlson who had been an assistant to animator Marc Davis. As Carlson recalled:

> Bob Carlson and I did the *How to Draw Donald Duck* book. John Lounsbery and I did the *How to Draw Mickey* book, and John Sibley did the *How to Draw Goofy* and *How to Draw Pluto*. Bill Justice and I did the *How to Draw Chip 'n Dale* one, and Jerry Hathcock and I did the *How to Draw Jiminy Cricket*.

In the same style was *Walt Disney's Tips on Animation* or for a premium price that book, two character guides, a flip book, a pressed wood animation table, pre-punched animation paper and more could be had in the *Walt Disney Animation Kit.*

In addition, guests could purchase four different flip books (Mickey Mouse, Donald Duck, Pluto, Chip'n'Dale) and twenty-six different postcards that referenced the Art Corner. Some of the postcards had a "squeaker" inside that made a noise when squeezed. There were funny signs, small little colored plastic television sets that when viewed through a small white hole in the back and a switch was pulled, the cartoon picture inside would rotate, six different decals with Disney characters dressed as artists and more.

Of course, guests could also purchase small sketch easels, pastels, brushes, berets (in black, red or green), a plastic palette with water color cakes, colored ballpoint pens with a gold Mickey Mouse and Disneyland logo, and pencils with the Art Corner logo.

At the back of the store, easels were set up where artists, including the Mickey Mouse Club Big Mooseketeer Roy Williams would do quick 18" by 24" sketches of the heads of popular Disney cartoon characters like Mickey, Goofy and Pluto.

Art of Animation Exhibit

MAY 1960—SEPTEMBER 1966

The Art of Animation exhibit was located between Circarama and the Art Corner. Previously, the space had been occupied by the Satellite View of America that had opened with the park.

When Walt Disney was producing the animated feature film *Sleeping Beauty,* he realized that a great way to publicize the "high art" approach of the film as well as address all the letters that flooded into the studio from young artists interested in animation would be to put together a traveling exhibit showcasing the history of animation as well as how animation was done.

Walt Disney created an exhibit showing the history and development of animation. He used elements from the film itself to explain the actual animation process. The traveling exhibit was entitled *The Art of Animation: A Walt Disney Retrospective.*

To put the exhibit together, Walt sent people to the animation "morgue" where the animation art was kept. Walt wanted some specific pieces and it wasn't just cel setups but backgrounds, concept art, story sketches, and more.

There were three versions of this exhibit and each featured different original art. In fact, a twenty-four page exhibit souvenir guidebook with a white cover was produced featuring material from the Bob Thomas book *The Art of Animation* (1958) also meant to publicize the film *Sleeping Beauty.*

One was showcased in Tomorrowland at Disneyland and it was natural to be placed next to The Art Corner that sold animation related material.

The exhibit in Tomorrowland featured early optical devices like thaumatropes and a zoetrope as well as displays explaining not only the history of animation but the process along the perimeter of the circular room. The interior of the room had plastic chairs, potted plants and ashtrays so guests could smoke.

Television monitors showed segments from the Disneyland weekly television show episode *The Art of the Animated Drawing* first shown on November 11, 1955.

There were two other traveling versions of the exhibit that toured the United States beginning in 1958 and then one was sent to be shown in Europe and the other to Japan in 1960 to once again promote the release of *Sleeping Beauty* in those countries.

In fact, the blurb for the attraction proclaimed:

> The Magic World of Walt Disney's Art of Animation. Animation through the ages...early motion picture uses...the first Walt Disney cartoon feature...sound and animation...how an animated cartoon is made today...the latest techniques in animation...This exhibit has been viewed by hundreds of thousands at showings in London—Paris—Tokyo—NOW—at Disneyland in Tomorrowland.

The famous attraction poster done by Paul Hartley also promoted that this was part of the "international exhibit" seen around the world. It was a popular exhibit because at the time very little was known about animation. It also served to help drive sales at The Art Corner next door. The expansion of the CircleVision theater next door in 1967 resulted in its removal.

Carousel of Progress
JULY 1967—SEPTEMBER 1973

The Carousel of Progress debuted in the General Electric pavilion for the 1964-65 New York World's Fair and when the fair finished it was transplanted into Tomorrowland at Disneyland.

Imagineer John Hench said:

> Carousel of Progress was inspired by Thornton Wilder's [play] *Our Town*. It was really quite a touching play. I saw it three times, I think. I came back and told Walt I thought that's what we should do for General Electric.

GE decided to fund the elaborate version of a similar concept that would feature an Audio-Animatronics family in different eras appreciating the advancements made by GE in a unique 240 seat theater where the audience seats moved around the perimeter of six stationary stages.

The transition to each new scene was accompanied by the show's theme song "It's a Great, Big Beautiful Tomorrow," written by the Sherman Brothers, in different musical styles to match each era.

While the audio-animatronics characters were simpler in movement than the President Lincoln figure at the Illinois pavilion, there were roughly thirty-two of them in the show that had to be coordinated, each on its own separate recording track.

The new Hench-designed Disneyland building was two-storied and there were two major changes to the show: First, the final scene was revised and updated, eliminating references to dated products like color kitchen lighting, and adding new miracles like videotape recording of television programs.

In the background, the Christmastime night showed the skyline of Walt's vision for Epcot with the Cosmopolitan Hotel towering in the center.

Second, as guests exited the show and went up the speed ramp, they no longer saw the *Skydome Spectacular* as they did at the fair, but an amazingly detailed miniature of Walt's dream for his proposed Epcot city.

However, with the death of Walt, the Disney Company was debating whether to pursue making that dream a reality so the city was re-dubbed "Progress City" to tie-in with all the references to progress in the attraction.

Built 1/8th of an inch to a foot, it was 6,900-square feet, 115-feet wide, and 60-feet deep. It had 2,500 moving vehicles (monorails, peoplemovers, moving sidewalks, electric trains), 20,000 trees, 4,500 structures (Walt insisted the interior of each of the buildings be finished, furnished and lit), 1,400 working street lights, and it all came alive as the audiences moved from one side of the room to the other on a three-tiered audience viewing area.

A small portion of that massive model was relocated to Walt Disney World where it could be seen from the Tomorrowland Transit Authority during part of its journey.

While the show entertained up to 3,600 guests each hour at Disneyland at its peak, dwindling audiences resulted in GE requesting the attraction be moved to Florida's WDW to expose their message to a new audience that never came to Southern California. The unique Disneyland theater became home to the America Sings attraction and later to the Innoventions exhibits.

America Sings
JUNE 1974—APRIL 1988

When the Carousel of Progress attraction left Disneyland for Walt Disney World, the innovative Carousel Theater where the audience seats rotated around the perimeter of six different stationary stages remained. Disney decided to develop a new show for that high capacity attraction where a new audience could be loaded every four minutes that would take advantage of the bicentennial festivities leading up to 1976. The theater was repainted red, white and blue.

The theater was also reformatted to revolve in the opposite direction since only the lower floor would be used and guests not transported to the upper level. That decision would later lead to an unfortunate tragedy. In July 1974 eighteen year old hostess Deborah Gail Stone was accidentally crushed to death between two walls as it transitioned to the next scene. It is unclear why she was in that position. Sensory lights for warning were then added as were walls that would breakaway if rotation was interrupted by something.

America Sings was designed by Imagineer Marc Davis as a nostalgic and patriotic salute to the history of music of the United States using audio-animatronics animals. Davis and Al Bertino selected the songs, avoiding any references to war and trying to find ones that might provide a humorous gag.

The show was hosted by Sam the Eagle voiced by folksinger Burl Ives along with his co-host, Ollie Owl voiced by Sam Edwards.

The first act takes place in the swamps of the early South. The second act was the plains of the Old West. The third act was in a big ballroom from the Gay Nineties. The fourth act is in a back alley by a subway entrance in the 20th century.

In addition there was a loading scene and an unloading stage with Sam and Ollie on a gazebo in the park. Sam singing a chorus of Yankee Doodle with special lyrics related to each era was the transition between each scene. In each scene, a weasel would pop up shouting "Pop goes the weasel".

Each stage was cleverly designed so that characters could rise up from the bottom or enter from either side with selective lighting defining a particular area so it seemed like a new location.

Songs included "My Old Kentucky Home," "Yankee Doodle," "Polly Wolly Doodle," "Down by the Riverside," "The Old Chisholm Trail," "Who Shot That Hole in My Sombrero," "Home on the Range," "Won't You Come Home Bill Bailey?", "Sweet Adeline," "I'm Only a Bird in a Gilded Cage," "Hound Dog," "Twistin' USA," and "Joy to the World."

After the bicentennial, attendance at the attraction started to decrease significantly and when Del Monte decided not to renew its sponsorship, it was closed. The building was used as office and storage space until it was redesigned as Innoventions in 1998.

Two of the geese with their exterior stripped off ended up as repair droids in the queue for Star Tours. Most of the other figures were installed in the new Splash Mountain. Neither Sam nor Ollie were relocated.

Captain EO

SEPTEMBER 1986—APRIL 1997

At a production cost of over twenty-three million dollars and sponsored by Kodak, the three-dimensional film experience *Captain EO* starring singer Michael Jackson opened at Disneyland on September 18, 1986, with additional versions opening in Walt Disney World, Tokyo Disneyland and Disneyland Paris.

Although built for *Captain EO,* Disneyland's Magic Eye Theater in Tomorrowland, that seated about 700 guests, originally opened in May 1986 with the amazing *Magic Journeys,* the original 3-D movie from Epcot's Imagination pavilion. Live theater special effects were added for the *Captain EO* presentation including lasers, fiber-optic stars, and fog effects that were all painstakingly synchronized with the action on screen.

The film was produced by George Lucas and directed by Francis Ford Coppola. A month after Michael Eisner took over as CEO of the Disney company in 1984, he invited Lucas to tour the Imagineering facilities in Glendale in hopes he would partner on some projects for the Disney theme parks.

Around the same time studio executive Jeffrey Katzenberg took Michael Jackson, who was a huge fan of Disneyland and visited often, around the same facility in hopes of generating a project.

Eisner said:

> We wanted to create a film like "Thriller" with Michael Jackson, who appealed to teenagers, but also to young kids, and even their parents.

Three different storylines were created and *Captain EO* (from the Greek Goddess of the Dawn) was selected. Rusty Lemorande scripted the film. Rick Baker provided the makeup. Jeff Hornaday did the choreography. Jackson himself wrote the two songs featured in the film: "We Are Here to Change the World" and "Another Part of Me."

Jackson starred as Captain EO, the leader of a spaceship's "rag-tag crew," which included a dwarfish, clumsy green elephant-like creature called Hooter; a small, long-tailed orange flying creature called Fuzzball; two conjoined creatures know as the Geex (Idy and Ody—also sometimes spelled Idee and Odee) who served as the navigator and pilot; and a robot security officer named Major Domo who had a smaller robot, Minor Domo, attached as a module to his back.

Commander Bog tells them to follow a "homing beacon" to a forbidding, dark industrial planet of sinister twisted metal and to give a gift to the Supreme Leader (Angelica Huston). Crashing on this foreboding looking world, the crew finds its way to the palace and are captured by her army and threatened with torture for their unauthorized visit. Fortunately, EO's music transforms the queen into a beautiful ruler and the entire world into a verdant paradise.

Most people found it more of an elaborate rock video than a film, especially with the interactive elements in the theater but it made no difference to the many rabid fans of Jackson.

Captain EO closed April 1997 at Disneyland and eventually at all the other Disney theme parks by August 1998. Eight months after Jackson's death, the film was brought back into the same theater as the Captain EO Tribute, once again sponsored by Kodak, and ran from June 2009 to June 2014.

Star Tours
JANUARY 1987—JULY 2010

When Star Wars creator George Lucas toured Imagineering head-quarters in Southern California, he thought the concept of using a motion-control simulator was an amazing opportunity to showcase his filmic universe.

The chosen storyline would be set just after the Rebel Alliance victory in the film *Return of the Jedi* (1983), which was the most recent film in the series at the time and one that many believed would be the final film.

To encourage intergalactic tourists to spend money in areas rebuilding after the conflict, a company called Star Tours is offering sightseeing excursions, with highlighted destinations including the forest moon of Endor, Hoth, Tatooine and Dagobah. R2-D2 and C-3PO are part of the Star Tours operation, having left military service at the end of the war with the Empire.

Lucas insisted that the attraction experience blend laughs and thrills, and he reportedly held the Imagineers in rapt attention as he acted out the entire story of the flight.

RX-24 or "Rex," an enthusiastic but inexperienced droid, was the pilot when the tour goes horribly wrong for the forty passengers in the StarSpeeder 3000 vehicle during the six minute flight. Actor Paul Reubens (better known as Pee Wee Herman) voiced the character because Disney was impressed with the work he did as the voice of the shipboard computer in the Disney film *Flight of the Navigator* (1986), as well as his ability to make panic comical.

The visionary Lucas spent hours guiding the fabrication and programming of the C-3PO audio-animatronics figure, whose outer shell was assembled from a box of spare parts sent from Lucas' Industrial Light and Magic team. The figure is authentic, as is the shell of R2-D2. Actor Anthony Daniels, who played the role of C-3PO in the Star Wars films and voices the figure in the attraction, visited several times to review the work.

Several prominent Imagineers and Industrial Light and Magic employees make cameo appearances, from the clever safety-procedures boarding video to the orange suited technicians seen on screen in the docking bay.

The Star Tours action was shot on 70mm film at a speed of 30fps to create clear, flicker-free images. The film was made "the old-fashioned way," with miniatures, models, motion-control cameras, optical printers and other techniques that were popular in Hollywood before the advent of computer-generated imagery.

That forbidding, twisting ice tunnel, for example, was constructed out of foam, with plastic-and-resin icicles along with clear blue resin. The "ice-teroid field" sequence took more than 28 hours to film as it included more separate elements than the most complicated special effects shot in *Return of the Jedi*.

The attraction that took over the building that formerly housed Adventure Thru Inner Space was always intended to have the film experience changed with new motions to match. In June 2011 Star Tours: The Adventures Continue opened with a new storyline and film but with several references to the original attraction.

Circarama

JULY 1955—SEPTEMBER 1966

Inspired by seeing a Cinerama presentation where three large screens were synchronized to show a motion picture, Walt Disney had Ub Iwerks develop a process where a movie could be presented on a series of screens that completely surrounded the audience. The two men share the patent on the process.

It was called Circarama not only as an allusion to Cinerama but also because the film was sponsored by the American Motors Corporation who produced cars like the Rambler. The building was located just to the left of the entrance of Tomorrowland.

The audience stood in an asphalt paved circular area forty feet in diameter with the eight foot high screens elevated about eight feet off the floor. There were no "lean" rails in those early days.

Eleven 16mm Cine Kodak Special cameras were mounted on a circular platform covering 360 degrees of arc that was strapped to the top of an American Motors Rambler station wagon to record *A Tour of the West* travelogue. Peter Ellenshaw was the art director and the filming was plagued by challenges.

There were three approximately twelve-minute showings of the film per hour with an intermission inbetween each for loading and unloading the theater.

The circular screen was divided by 6-inch wide vertical black strips into eleven 8-by-11 foot sections. The black separating panels added to the illusion of continuity between adjoining sections of the picture, because they eliminated the disturbing jiggle between adjacent screen sections as well as making it seem as if guests were in a car and looking out through the windows.

The sound was recorded on four magnetic channels and was fed into a bank of four 6-inch speakers mounted beneath each projector so the theater could be flooded with sound from all the speakers or distributed in a directional pattern in just one section.

A Tour of the West presented a journey beginning on Sunset Boulevard in front of the Beverly Hills Hotel, then a high speed trip down Wilshire Boulevard and then along the Los Angeles Freeways to Monument Valley, Arizona. The adventure continued through Newport Harbor in California (with the cameras mounted on a speedboat instead of the car) and then off to Las Vegas and the Grand Canyon.

The "race" down Wilshire Boulevard was filmed at half speed but projected at full speed creating the illusion of speed.

Ellenshaw said, "Suddenly we were racing down Wilshire at a hundred miles per hours, barely avoiding accidents, and crashing to a stop only inches from the cars in front, all with the sound of a police siren in the background. For guests, it was a virtual thrill ride."

In 1958, Walt created a brand new Circarama film for the Brussels World's Fair, *America the Beautiful*. The new film showcased portions of the entire United States. It was then shown at the American National Exhibition in Moscow, Russia in 1959. In June of 1960 the new film debuted at Disneyland sponsored by Bell Telephone as a free attraction.

CircleVision 360

JUNE 1967—SEPTEMBER 1997

Circarama had proven so popular with guests that the theater was extensively remodeled. It expanded into the building previously exhibiting Richfield's The World Beneath Us attraction next door to provide more capacity as part of the new 1967 Tomorrowland. It was also renamed Circle Vision 360 when Bell Systems took over the sponsorship of the new theater.

The film *America the Beautiful* that debuted in 1960 was a huge hit with guests.

So when the theater was expanded and updated, it was only natural that it be re-filmed to include in the immersive, somewhat futuristic-seeming circular theater.

The new pavilion was 34,000 square foot, serving 3,000 guests an hour and staffed by over forty-five hostesses from Bell to represent its company. During the pre-show, they narrated the evolution of Bell Systems. Then the guests were ushered into the eighty-foot diameter theater that had handrails that they could use for support during the eighteen minute show (nearly double the length of the previous film) that had been entirely re-shot in 35mm.

The show was now on nine screens rather than the previous eleven but once again encircled the audience high above eye level. The movement was so realistic that some guests got motion sickness when the scene tilted.

The new film included visits to Mount Rushmore, the White House, Mount Vernon, and Mount McKinley as well as a winding trip down Lombard Street in San Francisco, a cruise in Balboa Bay and many other fascinating sights that most guests had never seen.

After the film, guests filed through the exit doors into an area filed with interactive new advanced communictions equipment like the Picturephone where a guest could see the person they were talking to at three different locations around the country.

There were six family booths where an entire family could sit and talk at the same time to another person anywhere in the United States. There were even phones that children could pick up and hear a Disney animated character like Mickey Mouse on a recorded track talking to them.

Sponsorship changed over the years from AT&T until 1982 to Pacific Southwest Airlines (PSA) starting in 1984 which featured a new eight minute animated short pre-show *All Because Man Wanted to Fly* devoted to the history of aviation and space exploration and Delta Airlines beginning from 1989 until 1996.

In July 1984 the film was replaced by the new twenty-one-minute *American Journeys* in the afternoons and evenings while during the mornings *Wonders of China* made for the China pavilion at Epcot was shown. The two movies were run simultaneously until July 1996. *America the Beautiful* was brought back and continued to run until the pavilion's closing in September 1997.

In 1998, the pavilion became the waiting queue area for the very short-lived Rocket Rods attraction. A decade later it became the location for Buzz Lightyear's Astro Blasters attraction in November 2008.

The Disneyland Helicopter

JUNE 1955—AUGUST 1972

Since July 6, 1954, people had been able to take a helicopter from the Burbank airport to Anaheim in about a third of the time it would take by automobile. Walt Disney had taken such a flight and authorized the building of a heliport for Disneyland in 1955 that was located just outside of Tomorrowland near the Skyway station.

There were five helicopter flights daily from Los Angeles International Airport to Disneyland, taking approximately fifteen minutes. These flights were operated by Los Angeles Airways, a company that offered helicopter service to nearly a dozen southern California locations.

Private and military helicopters also made use of the site especially when bringing foreign dignitaries, celebrities and VIPs to Disneyland.

The one-way fare was roughly four dollars in 1955 but later increased to around $15 (although some airlines offered a massive discount to its passengers who wanted to add the service to their booked flight). Thousands used the service each year.

In 1960 the Disneyland Heliport was moved from the Disneyland Harbor Gate area to a parking lot annex on Winston Road, almost a mile away next to a golf drive range/parking lot. "Anaheim Disneyland Heliport" was a Transportation Center for buses/limos as well as L.A. Airways. The Tony Curtis movie *40 Pounds of Trouble* (1962) shows the characters boarding a helicopter for a trip to Disneyland.

Two major Disneyland-related tragedies occurred in 1968. The Disneyland/Los Angeles International Airport helicopter service suffered two of the worst civilian chopper crashes in U.S. history.

The first crash occurred on May 22, 1968, when N303Y was en route from Disneyland to LAX. At about 5:50 p.m., Flight 841 was flying near a Paramount dairy farm. A single missing bolt in the main rotor hub caused it to detach and struck the helicopter's fuselage and caused the other four rotor blades to go out of control. All 20 passengers who had spent the day enjoying Disneyland and the three-man crew were killed.

The second crash, on August 14, 1968, involved N300Y operating as Flight 417 from LAX to Anaheim. One of the main rotor head spindles failed due to metal fatigue and the attached rotor blade separated completely. The resulting imbalance sent the helicopter out of control and it crashed in Leuders Park, killing all 18 passengers and the three member crew.

The type of helicopter involved in both crashes was the Sikorsky S-61L that had a capacity of 28 passengers.

Local Anaheim motel owners had protested for years that the service was dangerous and the noise disturbed their guests. In January 1968, they had petitioned the Anaheim City Council to limit the flights but the Council sided with Disney that the value far outweighed the "minor disadvantages" to residents.

LAA suspended flights to Disneyland and went out of business in 1971. Golden West revived the helicopter service but ended it after five months in August 1972 and the bulldozed heliport became a parking lot for the Disneyland Hotel.

Disneyland Kids of the Kingdom
JUNE 1968—CIRCA 1985

In addition to hiring outside entertainment offerings for the park, Disneyland developed its own unique musical entertainment including the barbershop quartet called the Dapper Dans, the Coke Corner pianist as well as various groups for New Orleans Square among others.

The Disneyland Kids of the Kingdom first appeared in 1968, modeled after the Up with People! and Doodletown Piper singing groups popular at the time.

At Disneyland, fifteen perky, upbeat and clean-cut performers in their white outfits with red trim usually performed an approximately half hour show on the Tomorrowland Stage usually five times a day and sometimes on the movable Tomorrowland Terrace stage. Over the years, the basic outfits changed but were always matching and the group shrunk to eleven.

They recorded a record album on Vista Records in 1968 called *The Kids of the Kingdom: The Young Singing Stars of Disneyland* featuring nine songs from their repertoire. They were an integrated group with one pair of black performers.

Choreographer for the group was a young Barnette Ricci who later went on to direct the original Disneyland's Main Street Electrical Parade in 1972. Ricci also became the artistic creator and director of the original *Fantasmic!* in 1992 among many other credits. She started her Disneyland career as a dancer in the parades.

She eventually became vice president/show director of Special Events. She also directed the original Walt Disney World version of Kids of the Kingdom.

There is a video clip of the Kids of the Kingdom singing "This Land Is Your Land" on the March 22, 1970, episode of *The Wonderful World of Disney* titled "Disneyland Showtime," focusing on the opening of the Haunted Mansion hosted by Kurt Russell.

Executive Vice President of Walt Disney Entertainment Ron Logan recalled:

> Disneyland created an original genre stage show called the Kids of the Kingdom. A choice was made to bring together young talent because of availability, cost and image. It had a certain formula with about a dozen singer/dancers and an eight piece live band. The show was not advertised but was there as part of the atmosphere environment.

> The Kids of the Kingdom shows evolved through the years and eventually included Disney characters. There was a lot of discussion in those days as to whether that was appropriate. Time proved that it was not only appropriate but character-related stage shows became a major brand for the Disney parks.

In the 1980s, the group was the star of a stage show called *Disneyland Is Your Land* on the Tomorrowland Space Stage (built in 1977) celebrating the park's 25th anniversary. Each themed land in the park was highlighted through music, costumes and dance.

The group disappeared from Disneyland by 1985 but the Florida version of the group continued to perform at Walt Disney World through the end of the decade. Another version composed of an all Japanese cast appeared at Tokyo Disneyland for the first few years the park was open.

Acknowledgments

As always, I acknowledge not only the people who directly helped me with this specific book, but those who have inspired or supported me over the years. There are indeed angels in this world and I have been blessed to know so many of them in my life.

I would like to thank all the people who have bought my Disney history books because their continuing support has allowed this book to be published.

This book would not have been possible without the skills and encouragement of publisher Bob McLain and his Theme Park Press.

I acknowledge those sometimes unknown heroes of Disney history who have worked hard to keep the images and facts about extinct Disneyland alive for all of us:

- Werner Weiss (yesterland.com)
- Dave De Caro (davelandweb.com)
- David Eppen (gorillasdontblog.blogspot.com)
- Patrick Jenkins (matterhorn1959.blogspot.com)
- Chris Strodder, author of *The Disneyland Encyclopedia* (2017) and *The Disneyland Book of Lists* (2015).

Thanks to my brothers, Michael and Chris, and their families, including their children—Amber, Keith, Autumn, and Story. Also, thanks to my grand-nieces Skylar, Shea and Sidnee (Fairbanks) and grand nephews Max (Fairbanks) and Alex (Johansen). None of you read my books but all of you enjoy the Disney theme parks.

Thanks to all the original Disneylanders who were so gracious and generous sharing their memories with a wet-behind-his-ears eager kid who had endless questions as did several Imagineers. who also helped without hesitation. Now I am as ancient as all of you were.

Thanks to all the historians who have written about Walt's original Disneyland including Jeff Kurtti, Todd James Pierce, Dave

R. Smith, Donald Ballard, Randy Bright, Michael Broggie, Bruce Gordon, Kevin Kidney, Jack and Leon Janzen, David Mumford, Dave Mason, Tim O'Day, Jason Schultz, Robert Tieman, Jeff Pepper, Tom Tumbusch, Mark Eades, Scott Wolf, Chris Nichols and others who took the time to do the research and were generous in sharing it with the rest of us. You all have enriched Disney history for all of us and are a constant inspiration to try harder.

About the Author

Jim Korkis is an internationally respected Disney historian who has written hundreds of articles and over two dozen books about all things Disney over the last forty years. Jim grew up in Glendale, California, where starting at the young age of fifteen, he was able to meet and interview some of Walt's original team of animators and Imagineers.

Living less than an hour from Anaheim, Jim visited Disneyland many times as a child, a teenager and an adult and personally experienced many of the things in this book. The Disneyland he grew up with remains his favorite Disney theme park.

He accumulated fond memories of every visit and some well loved souvenirs including the Walt Disney Art of Animation Kit from the Art Corner and a Tinker Bell glow-in-the-dark wand. He authored the book The Unofficial Disneyland 1955 Companion (2016) covering the creation of Disneyland and its first full year of operation.

In 1995, he relocated to Orlando, Florida where he worked for Walt Disney World in a variety of capacities including Entertainment, Animation, Disney Institute, Disney University, College and International Programs, Disney Cruise Line, Disney Design Group, Disney Vacation Club, Disney Learning Center, and Yellow Shoes Marketing.

His original research on Disney history has been used often by the Disney Company as well as other organizations including the Disney Family Museum.

Several websites feature Jim's articles about Disney history:

- MousePlanet.com
- AllEars.net
- Yesterland.com
- CartoonResearch.com
- YourFirstVisit.net

In addition, Jim is a frequent guest on multiple podcasts as well as a consultant and keynote speaker to various businesses, schools and groups. He is not an employee of the Disney company.

To read more stories by Jim Korkis about Disney history, please check out his other books, all available from Theme Park Press:

- *The Unofficial Walt Disney World Companion 1971 (2019)*
- *The Vault of Walt: Volume 7, Christmas Edition (2018)*
- *Secret Stories of Mickey Mouse (2018)*
- *More Secret Stories of Disneyland (2018)*
- *Extra Secret Stories of Walt Disney World (2018)*
- *Call Me Walt (2017)*
- *Walt's Words (2017)*
- *Other Secret Stories of Walt Disney World (2017)*
- *Secret Stories of Disneyland (2017)*
- *The Vault of Walt: Volume 6 (2017)*
- *Gremlin Trouble (2017)*
- *Donald Duck's Daddy (2017)*
- *More Secret Stories of Walt Disney World (2016)*
- *The Vault of Walt: Volume 5 (2016)*
- *The Unofficial Disneyland 1955 Companion (2016)*
- *How to Be a Disney Historian (2016)*
- *Secret Stories of Walt Disney World (2015)*
- *The Vault of Walt: Volume 4 (2015)*
- *Everything I Know I Learned from Disney Animated Features (2015)*
- *The Vault of Walt: Volume 3 (2014)*
- *Animation Anecdotes (2014)*
- *Who's the Leader of the Club? Walt Disney's Leadership Lessons (2014)*
- *The Book of Mouse (2013)*
- *The Vault of Walt: Volume 2 (2013)*
- *Who's Afraid of the Song of the South? (2012)*
- *The Revised Vault of Walt (2012)*

About Theme Park Press

Theme Park Press publishes books primarily about the Disney company, its history, culture, films, animation, and theme parks, as well as theme parks in general.

Our authors include noted historians, animators, Imagineers, and experts in the theme park industry.

We also publish many books by first-time authors, with topics ranging from fiction to theme park guides.

And we're always looking for new talent. If you'd like to write for us, or if you're interested in the many other titles in our catalog, please visit:

www.ThemeParkPress.com

. . . .

Theme Park Press Newsletter

Subscribe to our free email newsletter and enjoy:

- Free book downloads and giveaways
- Access to excerpts from our many books
- Announcements of forthcoming releases
- Exclusive additional content and chapters
- And more good stuff available nowhere else

To subscribe, visit www.ThemeParkPress.com, or send email to newsletter@themeparkpress.com.

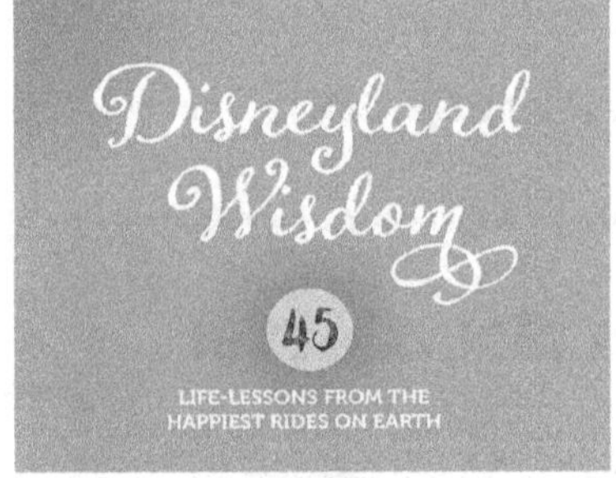

Read more about these books
and our many other titles at:

www.ThemeParkPress.com

www.ingramcontent.com/pod-product-compliance
Lightning Source LLC
Chambersburg PA
CBHW051527150726
47997CB00001B/419